Impulsive Dragon

Impulsive Dragon

Françoise Dewitt

authorHOUSE®

AuthorHouse™
1663 Liberty Drive
Bloomington, IN 47403
www.authorhouse.com
Phone: 1-800-839-8640

Published by AuthorHouse   04/04/2012

ISBN: 978-1-4678-7818-0 (sc)
ISBN: 978-1-4678-7819-7 (e)

"Forgetting ones ancestors is like being a brook without a spring, a tree without its roots"

PART ONE

1. Jade and Butterflies

Near Cu Nam, in the province of Quang Binh, Nguyễn Văn Kuyen, a cultured man, bought some rails and spent a fortune so that the train could reach his land. Nguyễn Văn Kuyen was Minh's uncle, whose famous ancestor was the Emperor Gia Long.

That line had not ascended to the throne because a son had died before his father, but Khuyen was still recognised in the village as someone of importance. His title was Hereditary Mandarin.

Amongst the dignitaries who were coming out of the house compound that evening, sitting comfortably in their brightly coloured sedan chairs, were other Mandarins and chiefs of different districts. Everyone had come to the grand opening of this "umbilical cord" which was putting an end to the isolation of their village.

This was the end of a day of much rejoicing and eating. The sun was painting the most delightful colours on the wispy clouds, forecasting a nice morning ahead. The upturned roofs of the houses were cutting out silhouettes on a sky that the last fires of a winter sun had majestically covered with crimson.

Nguyễn Văn Hao, himself Hereditary Mandarin and grandnephew of Emperor Tu Duc had been celebrating too and had just got back to his home when Minh found him in his study.

Hao, Minh's father, was quite tall and his complexion was not weather beaten but light. His long hair was piled up on the top of his head, as it was customary for people in high office ever since the Emperors. His personality was strong and honest, and the long black robe he was wearing that day gave him an imposing look. In his position of judge, he was feared but respected by all, several leagues around. Because he was reserved, he seemed cold, but he had a sense of irony and a biting sense of humour.

Minh often used to find him writing in this room, which he used with his two brothers to do their school work. He knew he had to wait in the doorway until asked to come in. Not daring to interrupt he waited patiently. The teaching of Confucius started singing in his head in a melodious whisper, "respect your parents always", and that is why none of Hao's five children would have dared question the authority of their father.

Minh was ten years old. He was the second of the three sons and the most boisterous too. Not very tall for his age but strong in body and in character, he would often find it very difficult to follow what his teacher had preached. His jet black hair was sprinkled with pink petals that morning, and looking like a hedgehog. It was cut above the ears and a fringe swept away from his inquisitive smiling eyes.
Minh straightened his clothes which were in disarray as he had not long before climbed a tree to get his kite untangled from the foliage in blossom.

"What it is?" The sharp tone of his father interrupted Minh's thoughts.

"May I come in father?" enquired Minh, startled by the sullen voice.

"Is it important? I'm rather busy!"

Minh tiptoed into the room and stood in front of his father who was sitting crossed legged on a low stool. In front of him a low table in dark shiny wood was laden with paper work.

"When can we go hunting again, father?"

"Maybe tomorrow, Minh, if I have finished here, and I won't be if I keep being interrupted! Why don't you go and talk to your mother!" Hao hadn't looked up from his papers and Minh knew that this was not a question but rather an order. He walked quickly towards the door again, taking shallower intakes of breath, in an attempt not to make a sound.

Hao had fifty people working in his rice fields and around his buildings. He also had twenty two dogs and some horses which he took hunting from time to time in the forest. Hunting was for the privileged few a way to pass the time, and Minh loved tiger hunting. He liked the feel of danger. He liked that little twisting in his stomach caused by fear and excitement mixed together and the whit involved in catching the king of their forest.

Although there were people to deal with meal times, Minh guessed that his mother would be in the kitchens, supervising and putting the finishing touches to the meal.

The kitchen quarters were set up away from the main buildings. This was to keep the smells away from the rooms where you would sit to work, relax and sleep. The cook would have a small room next to the kitchen he could call his own, with his sleeping mat, a small table and colourful cushions. Hao liked to look after his workers. He always said that if you looked after people, they would look after you.

Minh ran up the stony path and soon the aromatic smell of the pheu boiling away was mingling with the nutty aroma of sesame seeds frying in the pan.

"Mother, mother," shouted Minh even before he reached the building.

Suu came out. Her slim stature and her long black hair tied up on her head gave her a tall appearance.

Her face always looked radiant and her eyes, the colour of the purest jade, were always smiling. Her arms were as slender as the neck of the cranes that you could see embroidered on her tunic.

"What's the matter, Minh!" she sang out.

"I'm bored; can you tell me a story?"

"Oh, is that all . . . what sort of story now?" smiled Suu, who was used to her second son's inquisitive mind.

"Tell me again about when you met father please," pleaded Minh.

"Ok," sighed Suu, "let's go and sit under the orange tree. We might as well be comfortable. They are doing all right in the kitchen."

As they sat close to each other, a warm breeze teased some of the white flowers from the branches above them, like fragranced snow-flakes. The evening was warm. Suu began quietly, as if reminiscing just for herself.

"When your father was of marrying age, the custom was that his parents would found him a wife befitting his social rank and religion. He also needed a wife who would be able to look after the running of his house and would know how to receive his guests. A wife changes family when she gets married, you know," added Suu looking at her son, nodding.

"That's terrible!" exclaimed Minh, "anyway, I'm never going to get married!"

"Well, I didn't want to leave my parents, but I had to do as I was told. That is the way things are," explained his mother.

"Is it true that you are older than father?" ventured Minh with a cheeky look on his face. "You don't look it," he hastily added.

Suu smiled. "Yes, if a wife is a bit older than her husband, a Chinese proverb says that the rice will be plentiful, so people think it would bring good luck. That is why often the girl is promised to the boy's family even before he is born and they usually marry when they are about fifteen years old."

"Did you marry at fifteen then?" asked Minh, his voice showing his amazement.

"Actually I was eighteen and your father was sixteen," replied Suu. "Your grand parents sent a dowry over, well before the wedding day. There was some jade jewellery, which is supposed to represent all that is perfect in human nature, high collared robes and other silk clothes and china kitchenware."

"But if you were "promised" before you were born, does that mean that you didn't know father before you got married then?" frowned Minh, puzzled. Every time he listened to that story it seemed that more and more questions popped into his head. It was as if he was listening to it for the first time again.

"I knew your father by sight, but I didn't know at first that it was him my parents had chosen for me, I knew that he was the Mandarin who lived in Cu Nam. We had a lot of respect and admiration for him because we had heard that he was always fair and honest, but I had never spoken to him, because a girl should not talk to strangers. I rarely went out of the house anyway and never without a chaperone."

"So did you want to marry him then, if you knew him a little bit? What is a chap . . . thingy you have to take with you when you go out?"

Suu smiled. "A chaperone is somebody who goes out with you. A friend maybe, so you are not on your own." Then she added getting closer to his ear and with a knowing look on her face, "really they are there to spy on you. If you do something you shouldn't do, like talk to strangers, they might remind you that you shouldn't, or they might tell on you . . ."

"Oh! Like my friend Truong, when we go to town together."

"Well . . . not quite! Anyway, marriage was the last thing on my mind! One day," Suu carried on, still smiling at her son's naivety "my parents said: Suu, it is time for you to get married, we have chosen your husband. I was devastated. I didn't want to leave home. I thought about all the things I was used to and everything I would have to leave behind to go and live with strangers, a very daunting prospect! Both sets of parents, your grandparents, became good friends but that did not change my mind. I was secretly hoping that they would change their mind, but that would never happen."

"Why not mother?" exclaimed Minh. "Why couldn't they change their mind?"

"Because once you promise, you cannot go back on your word. It would be a great dishonour," explained his mother. "My mother told me that parents have their children's interest in mind and that if both parties have similar values, everything would be good, so I didn't question her anymore."

"What does that mean, "similar values"?"

"It means similar beliefs, in religion but also in the way of doing things. Your father's family had a good reputation for being honest people and also well educated, so there was a chance that your father was a good person well matched with the way my family did things. That meant that we would get on well."

Minh cuddled up to his mother. He felt so good when they were together. He could smell her sweet jasmine perfume emanating from her long green robe.

Suu continued, "One noon, my mother was busy in the kitchens and I asked her what was happening. Everybody was rushing in and out of the building and there was a feel of celebration in the air. I could see that from all the flower displays and the coloured ribbons and tissue paper banners. "Suu," she said, "go and put your prettiest tunic on and put some flowers in your hair, your fiancée Hao is coming to meet you today.""

"Was it your wedding day?" inquired Minh. "Were you afraid?"

"No, that was the day before the wedding. It is customary for the bride's parents to invite the future groom to dinner the day before the wedding," continued Suu. "So the table was prepared with embroidered decorations of butterflies, for marital happiness, mandarin ducks, for marital fidelity, and bats for good fortune. My wedding dress had been made in red satin because red is the colour of felicity."

Suu's voice trailed off dreamily, remembering and reciting what her mother had explained to her that day.

"Mum . . ." whispered Minh, as if he didn't want to wake her, but he still had so many questions dancing in his head he couldn't help himself and started to pull on her long silky sleeve. "What is felicity?"

But Suu did not hear him.

"I was really worried that day. I knew the day when I would have to leave my family was near. I would have to please a new mother and I had heard stories of mother in laws using their son's wife as their servant."

"What happened next?" said Minh with a worried look on his face as if he were reliving the terrible ordeal together with his mother, although really he knew everything had been fine in the end. His grandmother had been his idol ever since he had been able to walk to her house on his own.

"Well, that afternoon, after the customary formalities and greetings were done, I dared set eyes on him, your father. It was not proper for the bride to be, to look at her fiancée in the eyes, but I couldn't help myself. And guess what . . . it was him, I recognised him, the mandarin's son I had noticed before on my walks and for whom I had felt a secret attraction I had thought forbidden."

Minh and Suu smiled at each other. All was well, and a feeling of being at peace enveloped them both as they stayed for a while in each others arms, surrounded by a soft pink and white carpet of delicate blossoms.

Minh wanted every day to be like this. He liked his secret weekly adventures outside the compound but he also knew that he could easily reach the safety of his father's land, which spread for a few miles around and this surely would last forever.

2. The Old and the New

Hao stormed into the kitchens.

"Tea, quick, and make sure it's not too hot!" he demanded. In no time the cup was presented to him. Hao put his lips to the brim to taste the steamy liquid.

"Go and get me a knife!" he blurted, his cheeks suddenly as red as his robes.

The cook was a short man, who looked like a beer barrel. His head was as bald as a coot and his ears were sticking out like two handles on a vase.

He quickly ducked towards the wall, rubbing his hands together as if to wipe away the sting of the lash he thought he was bound to receive.

"A knife, to scrape the hairy skin of the pig with this boiling water you have just brought me!" shouted Hao as he slammed the cup down onto the table, leaving a pool of the yellow liquid that the wooden table drank avidly. Then he left without waiting for another drink to be prepared.

Minh, who was gathering some flowers in the garden with his mother, looked at her. Hao's voice could be heard above the surrounding noises. The five brothers and sisters, especially the boys were very worried when Hao had outbursts like this one. That meant that his mood would stay like this for a while and he would be stricter than he already was.

Minh thought about "the little black book". Hao would mark down the amount of infringements to the rules they had committed and at the end of the week they would be whipped with a bamboo stick, or asked to kneel for two hours in the middle of the yard so everyone could see how bad they had been.

Minh, who was always full of mischief, had felt on many occasions the sharp gravel digging into his knees and the sting of the stick onto his bottom, when he had not had time to put some padding into his trousers.

One time, when he had been playing with his mates' dried clay marbles, one of them had hit his teacher's head and he had had to run away. He winced as he remembered it now. He could still hear the popping noise it had made on impact. He could still see the teacher's surprised face, followed by the fury in his eyes. He could also feel the bamboo whip digging in his posterior, when after having run for a while and thinking he was safe, he had ventured back into the classroom only to find his father waiting for him behind his desk.

"Don't worry," said Suu patting him on the back, "nothing that a good meal won't fix," and she strutted quickly towards the building to hurry the cook.

Minh walked towards the main house. He skipped through the orange trees, passed the pond, where precious fish danced all day long, playing with the bubbles spurting out of a fountain, which never stopped singing. Beyond was the yard where the main house spread in a long one-storey building surrounded by a peristyle.

Minh went in through the ornate sliding door. Along the circular corridor were several openings to different rooms. Columns made of precious woods like mahogany, magnolia or jack held a tiled roof with upturned corners. In the main room was a water clock decorated with golden dragons, stretching the thread of time as would an hourglass.

Minh loved this room. He liked the soothing sound of the water as each bubble burst on landing, rippling the surface of the crystal clear liquid. In the distance, coming from the stables, he could hear the barking of the dogs and the hoofs of the horses knocking on the cobbled stones. Minh peered out of the window. Everything seemed quiet except for some banging past the stables where some workers were busy building another house.

Minh remembered his father telling him that he was building a house for each of the boys.

"Each house has been carefully planned following feng shui."

"What is Feng Shui father?" he had asked.

"It is the Chinese art of determining the best position of a building, so that it will bring good fortune to those who live in it. To maximise harmony between wind and water elements, the front of the house has to face South, because South is sunshine and fortune. Listen carefully, you might have to do the same for your children one day," Hao had said. "The back must face North to fend off winds and enemies. When it is time for you three boys to get married you will stay near the family home, but still keep your independence as custom dictates."

Even Minh's bride had been chosen, but that he didn't know yet—that was the last thing on his mind.

The banging in the background made Minh remember the day when one of the carpenters had been chastised by his father for his shoddy work.

Hao had shouted in his usual sarcastic voice, "Did you need some fire wood then!" and the worker had to redo the piece that did not match properly.

"Why was his father so grumpy all the time?" Minh thought to himself, was it because he was worried, as his mother had said to him before? Worried about what? Life seemed so peaceful here, so uneventful, so boring, he thought.

Sometimes his father would surprise him and take him outside the grounds. This was usually as a reward for good school work. Minh was mischievous, but in no way had bad results at school. He was very clever at Mathematics and Chinese, and this, his father had drummed into him, was very important for his future.

With his father was not the only time Minh had actually been out of the compound of course. He had escaped several times without anyone noticing. On these occasions he had felt this delicious feeling, a subtle mixture of satisfaction and fright, which transforms itself into a sort of euphoria. It was how one felt, when usually respectful of the rules one dares, after some deliberation, to disobey.

Minh knew only too well that these escapades had to be kept secret. His father would not have been impressed, since the rules had always been that no one was to leave without his permission, "and where was the excitement in that?" he thought to himself. Although he had enjoyed a visit to Hue with Hao at the end of term last year, when his father had promised to take him to a French restaurant there, Minh had been surprised at all the different food and the different people and language he had not been accustomed to.

He had tasted a ruby liquid and had asked his father, "Why do they drink vinegar?"

Looking around the restaurant room, he had noticed strange people with hairy faces and loud voices. They spoke with such animation and punctuated everything with abrupt gestures. They were looking at others boldly and had an unrestrained manner with women.

All this, he had thought at the time, was in great contrast with the reserved manners he had been told to adopt in public places. Politeness was almost to the point of obsequiousness. Eating a tiny mouthful at a time from the end of sticks and drinking in minute cups was the way it had been for generations.

These foreigners seemed "uncouth and immoral", as his father had called them, yet Minh had heard that things were changing because of them. People were gradually modifying their way of life and their way of eating. You could now find a lot of imported goods like potatoes and other vegetables and fruit, and the less complicated French way of cooking was catching on.

Minh thought it was not all bad. Surely it was a good idea to take some things from the new and some things from the old to create a good balance in life.

Minh sat on one of the cushions near the clepsydrae and let the water tickle his fingers. He should have been working on his Chinese writing but he didn't feel like it.

One day he had said to his father: "Why can't I go to the French school like some of my friends?"

"Because I don't agree with the way the French are doing things," had replied Hao. "I'm not having you reciting "our ancestors the Gauls", he had laughed ironically. "They've already given us a new alphabet, now they want to poison our morals!"

Minh's school was on his father's land where Hao employed teachers himself. These teachers were living there and were regarded as part of the family. They were chosen carefully as Hao thought a good educator would help his children value the way of life he believed in, by exalting the old values and depreciating the new. He believed their young romantic spirit would be easily aroused. He had explained all this to his sons, but Minh was not convinced that this was the way forward. How would learning all those numerous characters help him in life? Chinese was used in the old Annam and took years to learn.

"Because of the amount of characters, which are as numerous as human ideas," his teacher had said, "scholars spend a life time perfecting the art of writing. Some know how to speak it and some only how to write it."

"The new way of writing is so much easier," had ventured Minh.

"This is not the point. This new way is causing the falling in the study of Chinese characters, then what next? All that our ancestors have lived by will be forgotten? Unthinkable! Remember, to break away from the teachings of our ancestors is to break away from tradition and in doing so, break away from our whole past, our roots. Filial devotion, fidelity and hierarchy, that has been our way since the Emperors. The French teach their children about equality of rights and about people who have risen against their kings. Their children learn about glorified sensibilities and passions and hear stories about unfaithful wives and sons who put love before filial devotion . . ." his teacher had carried on.

Minh had been surprised to hear his teacher talk with such passion. He knew his father had chosen this little old man with a broken back, whose smile let you discover a worn out set of teeth, because he was from the "old school". His father was against the new political regime, but Minh did not understand exactly why.

Suddenly Minh heard some voices coming from the direction of the house. He had been so deep in thought that he had forgotten where he was. He quickly hid behind one of the pillars, crouching on the stone floor and making himself as small as he could. Some important looking men started coming in, folding their sunshades on the door-step and leaving them near their sandals in a well organised line, creating a festooned border around the entrance. Their dark robes were swinging with a silky rustle. Their neat plait forming like ebony egg on the top of their head.

Minh held his breath. He noticed that his older brother Thao was there, followed by his father. His brother was tall and slim and looked much older than him. He had not been part of their games for a while now and was always studying or in meetings with his father.

Minh really felt that he shouldn't have been there. He tried to make himself small and hoped his dark clothes would merge into the shadows that invaded this part of the room behind the water clock.

The cook entered with several neatly laid out dishes on a tray and displayed them on the table. The guests started eating from the plates passing them in a circular motion on a Lazy Susan in the middle of the ebony table. Minh could smell the imperial rolls, the mince dumpling you had to cook yourself in the pot of boiling water, the pheu where the aromatic herbs were mingling with the noodles and his stomach started to call out. "Thank goodness for the noise of the water" he thought to himself.

A heated discussion started between Hao and one of the professors. Although Minh could only pick out some of the words, he understood that it was one of those meetings which no one was allowed to talk about outside the compound.

Minh knew that Hao's job as a Mandarin was to look after two sorts of lands, his own and some land belonging to the district, mostly rice fields. He employed many people to work these fields and would keep a certain amount of the crops for himself and his family. The rest was to be distributed around the district. This job, Minh understood, would need his father to be strict with people and to have meetings with other Mandarins like himself.

Hao was also Doctor in Chinese writing and Head of the Oriental Culture School he had opened. Also and more importantly, he was very often involved in political meetings, which were held in the main house. This was obviously one of these, thought Minh as he tried to comprehend what was going on.

"Several attempts have been made to achieve moderate reforms with the cooperation of the colonial regime, but everything has been rejected once again!" stated one of the scholars.

"We need to overthrow this government!" shouted another.

"If we need to use violent methods, then so be it!" quietly added Hao, looking around the table for nods of agreement.

"We need to restore the Dynastic Order, that's what we need," added an elderly man at the other end of the table.

"You are probably right, but I can't see that happening. That's why I don't disagree completely with what we have now. I just think we should have more say in what's happening in our own country!"

"That's right, lack of equality is the problem here!"

"You've said it, an equal share in the running of this country is not much to ask for. We are fed up with being regarded as inferiors by these strangers," piped in Thao.

"Come to think of it we've tolerated them long enough. If they don't want to regard themselves as guests and act as such, then I say kick them out."

"They have taken away the dignity of this country. We must fight to get it back . . .

Minh woke up with a start. He was alone once again. On the table the remnants of the dinner beckoned him. Gingerly he approached the deserted plates. He was starving. Tucking into an half emptied bowl of rice, he wondered what all these talks had been about.

3. Grandmother's Little Devil

"Let's go for a walk!" Minh decided, addressing his friends and Tuy his younger brother, who had arrived for school that morning. "Come on you lot, we've got a few minutes before class starts. We can't be wasting this sunshine," he declared.

"I'll go and ask teacher to make sure it's OK," said Truong his best friend, who was a little less impulsive than he was. Truong ran towards the school building, while Tuy just stood there expectantly.

Minh had known Truong ever since they were babes in arms. Both mothers had been neighbours and had kept in contact even after they had married. Truong was a good influence on Minh. Suu had noticed several times before, that he was like a brake on the reckless mind of her son. Many times he had stopped him from doing something that would have caused trouble or even worse an accident.

Truong was taller than Minh, a little bit plump, as his weakness was the sesame seed cakes that Minh's grandmother often sent to the school as a treat to the boys. He was also three years older, hence the wiser temperament, which often made his friend smile and mockingly call him "prof".

After a few minutes, Truong came running back.

"It's ok, but we must make sure we are back for our lesson in an hour," he said puffing as if he had just run a mile and bent forward holding on to his knees.

"Yes, of course, we'll be back," assured Minh, who although he respected his teacher for his knowledge was not really bothered about what he had said on this occasion.

The three lads walked down the dusty road kicking the stones nonchalantly.

Tuy started picking some of the grass which was growing along the hedge of the path and making screeching noises with it. They laughed noisily and shouted at a stray dog which came sniffing on their heels.

As they arrived near the village, they came to a market. The crowd was a multicoloured mass. Women crouched near their baskets full of wares were shouting towards prospective buyers the praises of their fruit, their meat, the cakes they were cooking on a makeshift stove. Others were draping themselves in the silk they were displaying in an attempt to entice someone into buying. The noise was a deafening song, which only they could understand as they were competing with their neighbours for the attention of anyone around. The crowd opened to let pass a group of Buddhist monks in their saffron yellow robes. Their heads were shaven, and their skin light. Their slanted eyes gave them a mischievous look mixed with kindness, which earned them the trust of most people.

"If you are generous towards these monks, you will surely gain paradise," said an old lady to the woman on the next stall, as she was filling a bowl full of rice for one of them.

"It is good Karma," nodded the other.

The boys started running between the stalls like caged up animals suddenly discovering the euphoria of freedom. They seemed to have sprouted wings and went from one table to another, skipping and dancing under the amazed glare of the stall-holders. From behind their ware of almonds, mushrooms and bright coloured silk the store keepers changed their initial stare into frowns and gestures, punctuated with insults.

Minh and his friends just laughed as they ran off into a neighbouring street. There they met up with Lao, who was just on his way to school.

"You are a bit late!" exclaimed Minh.

"I know, I had to help my mother set up her market stall." Lao's father had died in an ambush, they had heard. Although they did not understand quite what had happened exactly, they had not dared ask any questions. Now Lao was the man of the family and found it very difficult to adjust to his new life. He was torn between still acting like a teenager and being a man, looking after his mother and his two sisters. Hao had told him that he was still welcomed at the school whenever he wanted to have a change from his duties at home. He believed that you were never too old to learn and that of course you never stopped learning.

Suddenly Minh noticed an enormous snake wrapped round a stone well. He quickly grabbed a stick and started hitting the beast. Truong, Tuy and Lao, the one they called "cautious one", kept away at a safe distance.

"Leave it!" shouted Lao, "You don't know if it is poisonous!"

"Don't worry," laughed Minh, "he won't be able to reach me, he is not fast enough!"

"I think Cautious One is right," said Tuy, "you are asking for trouble!"

"You baby!" said Minh shaking his head at his brother, "what do you think Truong? It's a beauty isn't it?"

"I think it is time to get back actually, come on you lot-we don't want to be late," his friend stated hoping Minh would agree.

"Go on, you start off, I won't be long," Minh answered, pocking the animal on the head.

"I'm not a baby," sulked Tuy while following Truong.

The boys started running towards the school playing catch at the same time. Soon they were out of sight. Minh could not hear their laughter anymore. All he could hear was the singing of the crickets in the tall grass. He tried to catch one of them, which appeared particularly big. He was rushing around ruffling the weeds around him without success as the little creature carried on dancing from leaf to leaf without showing any sign of tiredness. Minh suddenly collapsed with exhaustion. He laid there for a while on his bed of cool grass, loosing himself in the immensity of a deep blue sky.

A slow movement attracted his attention to the well again. The snake was on the move. Minh took out his pocket knife and dug it into the almond shaped head. Some pinky substance started spurting out and the long body became limp, sliding off its perch. Minh grabbed the reptile by the tail and started dragging it behind him towards his father's fields. The skin would make a beautiful pouch, he thought. As he arrived within listening distance of the school building, he realised that the lesson had already started without him. He noticed his father standing near the doorway, one fist on his hip the other holding a stick.

"The devil is back," shouted Hao brandishing the bamboo rod as he spotted him. "Always have to have his own way!"

Minh let go of the yellow snake and started running towards some bushes on the other side of the yard. From his hiding place he could see all his friends coming out of the school room and admiring his catch. He smiled with pride and decided to settle down for a snooze. His father was bound to have other things to do. He wouldn't bother waiting for too long or even coming after him—he was sure of it. He probably wouldn't forget about it though, but Minh thought he could deal with that when it came to it. This great boa, which was taller than a man would provide a feast of rich meat for everybody in the village.

When he woke the sun was high. Everything was quiet. He noticed that school had ended and pupils and tutor were asleep under the orange trees, having their afternoon nap. Minh wondered what mischief he could get up to now. He went to the farmyard and picked up some black hen's droppings.

"This is the right choice," he whispered to himself, a grin on his face, "black hen is particularly smelly" he added creasing his nose.

Slowly he walked back to the school yard, then towards the sleepy teacher, paying attention not to make too much noise with the gravel crunching under his feet.

Then he delicately put the smelly drops he had held softly between his fingers into his teacher's nostrils.

The man woke up with a start, and screamed as if he had just been bitten from head to toe by a colony of red ants. He was treading the ground as if there was red hot charcoal under his feet. He looked like a puppet and someone was working his strings.

Minh didn't stay to find out the consequences of his action and took refuge at his grandmother's. He was still giggling that evening when she put him to bed.

"You are naughty Minh," she said leaning over him, "when will you act a little bit more sensibly? You do sometimes, so you can do it. Do you remember last year?"

Minh lay on his sleeping mat. He recalled the typhoon season of the previous year when everything was flooded for miles.

"Thank goodness our houses are safe on high ground," his father had said to them.

"But the neighbouring farms are not so lucky," his mother had answered.

He had climbed to the top of a tree and could see cattle swimming underneath him, mooing in despair as they were treading the water, desperately trying to get a foot-hold. Their eyes seemed like saucers as they stared in an amazed glare. A woman was crying and whining that she could not save her buffalo. He had taken the bit of rope he had in his pocket tied round his knife, and slid down towards the water. He had started swimming towards the scared bovine while the woman had cheered him on, waving towards the animal. Finally he had reached the buffalo and tied the rope round its neck then swam back towards the bank where the lady was standing, her feet deep in mud.

"Minh where have you been?" had enquired his mother.

"I've been helping a woman with her buffalo. She said she had nothing left of her crop and now she was about to lose her animal."

"That was kind Minh. What would you do if one day you were alone," had said his mother. "What would you do for food if everything was gone from the fields?"

"I would go to the loft," he had answered surprised, "there is always plenty of rice up there."

A week passed without incident and Minh had walked back home.

Then during one school break, the boys were playing in the yard.

"I feel peckish," declared Minh. "Let's climb the orange tree! I'll shake the branches," he added to his friend Truong as he started his ascent, "get ready to catch."

Truong had no time to warn him. The fruit came down in a sudden avalanche filling the well with a muffled noise. The children stood there open mouthed.

"Your father will be livid!" exclaimed one of them.

"Yes, and here he comes!" shouted Tuy.

Hao appeared, a stick in his hand, but Minh had climbed too high and Hao could not reach him. Undeterred Hao turned towards one of the outbuildings. Minh kept his eyes on him, apprehensive. What would his father do? Hao hadn't said a word but Minh didn't believe he had got away with this.

Sure enough, Hao came back followed by his uncle and he was brandishing an axe. The uncle was talking vehemently and was trying to hold the angry man back. Minh thought better not wait any longer and as fast as a lizard scurried to the bottom of the tree and ran once again to his grandmother's house. There he climbed onto the roof to keep an eye on the path for any sign of his father.

After a while, which seemed like hours to him, he climbed back down as fast as he could, worried that his father might be waiting for him round the corner. He quickly entered the house to greet his grandmother.

"This time I'd better not go home for a couple of weeks, grandmother," he managed to say in between two breaths.

"You've got too much energy, Minh" she declared.

"Yes, I would really like to do judo but father thinks I am too boisterous," he stated as Grandmother was making him sesame sweets and coconut ribbons, and although he knew he didn't deserve it, he could not refuse such treats.

"You know he has forbidden it," she answered keeping her eyes on the sweet mixture.

"Mother, thinks it is useful knowledge for self-defence, so uncle is giving me some lessons. You won't tell will you?" he said hastily, although he knew that his secret was safe.

"What will happen if you have an accident? He will find out then!"

"I've already broken my finger, but mother told me to soak it in vinegar and it's better now," said Minh munching on the coconut pieces.

Grandmother shook her head, smiling. Her many years were etched on her kind face, where two sparkling eyes were always smiling at you. She was small and bent and from time to time when she faltered Minh had to hold her arm which seemed so skinny that he was worried he might break it.

He loved his grandmother. She only had kind words to say to people. In fact all the children in the village loved to visit and she would make them Mongolian Hot-pot, a dish where you cook your own slithers of meat in the boiling water placed in the middle of the table, then dip them in your own tiny dish of spicy sauce. When it was time to go home, she would wrap lots of different sweets in tissue paper for them to take home, though very often these would not last that long.

These were unconcerned childhood days, but doesn't happiness exist only in parallel with misfortune?

4. A lesson to be learnt

Grandmother would always have some tale to recount her young visitors and this was the reason why they would very often come when they should have been at school.

That morning as she was sweeping her door-step, she noticed that Minh was sitting awkwardly on the edge of a small parapet on the bank of the small river where she could always get her daily supply of fresh water.

Her house was smaller than theirs and older looking, but the surroundings were idyllic. The sandy path that reached the front door led you over a small wooden bridge that was painted red and gold. It lay over the stream where clear water had polished the stones that spread in its bed. Mosses and small fragranced flowers grew along the banks, forming like a delicate frill.

"Hello! What are you doing here instead of being at school?"

"I broke my leg; father said I could have the day off today, as we were so late back yesterday."

"How did you do that? What do you mean "late back?""

"I broke it at judo! Mother had to tell father because she said it was an "open fracture", which is very bad," declared Minh proudly. "So we went to the French Hospital because father thought they would have better equipment for that sort of thing, but they wanted to amputate, that means cut my leg off!"

"I know what it means!" exclaimed grandmother, her face reflecting her worry.

"So we came back home and father was very angry at the French doctors. He said that his friend Doctor Li would deal with it. Doctor Li bandaged it very tight and I am not supposed to walk on it."

"Then what are you doing coming here when you should be in bed!" she said rushing in to bring him lots of brightly coloured scatter-cushions and helping him down gently onto them under the porch.

"I got bored."

Only a minute passed before Minh's racing mind came up with a question.

"Grandma, why is our country always at war?"

Grandma left the broom against the wall and sat down on the first step near her grandson.

"I think because people always want what they haven't got. They then try to take it from someone else. Greed always causes arguments. People are too close to material things. They should listen to the Buddha! . . . but what makes you ask this question?"

"Something I heard father say to Thao."

"You know, you shouldn't be listening to other people's conversation, you might find out more than you bargain for."

"I only heard it by accident, honest grandma," whined her favourite grandson, who knew that she was not really upset with him.

"Are you comfortable?" she asked as she padded the cushions around his back. "I will tell you a story that my mother told me years ago. It was during the war with China, all our young men had gone to fight, a heroic song on their lips, happy to serve their country, but sad too because they had to leave their families, wives and children.

Over in a small village a couple was living a peaceful life. They were expecting a child and were extremely happy, but soon Thai the husband had to go to war. The poor woman could not bear the separation and spent her days crying. Soon after she had a little boy, who as soon as he could speak would ask:

"Where is father?"

The poor mother could not answer him as she did not truly know where her husband was or when he would get back. She tried to put these questions at the back of her mind by working harder and harder each day, but the child would not let her forget.

One evening, when darkness had fallen, the lamp cast a shadow on the wall. A good idea came to her. To sooth her child she pointed to it and said:

"Darling, father is coming today, look!"

The trick succeeded and the child did not worry her again with his questions.

The sight repeated itself every night. The boy laughed at the sight of the shadow moving on the wall, and his mother felt happy too to have found a metaphor for her love. For her, love, like the shadow, never gave up. It never gave her a moment's rest.

She neglected herself. Having no appetite, she lost a lot of weight and became the shadow of her former self.

The mournfulness, which consumed her was fed with the continual fire of the memories of things they had done together. Did her husband, who was so far away, have any idea about this fever that consumed her? Did he know the depth of her feelings, she wondered. Where they had led such idyllic moments, where felicity had smiled on them, now everything seemed to have turned against them. Often she had wished she could delude herself as she had deceived the child!

At last one fine morning in spring, Thai appeared on the threshold. What happiness to be together again! What elation! Thai rushed to the child he had not seen yet, but to his surprise the little boy refused to kiss him.

"You are not my father," he would say again and again.

"Because you have never seen me you do not recognise me!" sighed Thai, "You will soon get used to your father."

"You are not my father," repeated the child. "Father will come only at night, and only leaves me when I fall asleep."

Thai was shocked. His wife had a lover!

"Adulteress! You betrayed me while I only had thoughts for you!"

Blind with jealousy, he refused to hear any explanations. He sent her back to her mother, which was a great dishonour for a married woman.

His wife suffered from the glares of strangers. She knew she had been faithful and her friends knew it too, but they didn't know how to prove it to the doubting husband.

In the end under the weight of despair she drowned herself in the river.

Thai lived alone with the child. Although he could not forgive, he still loved her and longed for her.

One evening, night came suddenly and Thai deep in his thoughts had not noticed. His child frightened of the sudden darkness started to cry for the light. Thai lit up the lamp and tried to amuse the boy with his shadow.

"Here comes father!" Here comes father!" exclaimed the child. "Look on the wall!" He is here at last! Every time mother wants to look at him she lights up the lamp and he comes immediately. Can you see him now?"

Thai could see. He could see clearly now but it was too late. He understood and was tortured with remorse and overcome with grief."

When Grandmother stopped, Minh sat there for a while.

"It is a very sad story," he finally said. "What a stupid husband!"

"War is a very sad thing. It destroys everything . . . but, let's not get morose, do you want another story?"

"Yes, please. I could listen to you all day, Grandma. This is better than struggling with my Chinese writing."

On the surface of the river he noticed some dragonflies skilfully weaving up and down, as close as they could to the surface of the water. A fat carp, waiting for the opportunity of a good meal, was jumping from time to time, leaving behind her a trail of droplets shining like diamonds in the morning sun.

"Look at that fish!" he exclaimed clapping his hands.

"Here is a story that is a little bit more fun. See what you think," grandma carried on.

"Once upon a time there was a monk, who like all other religious men, was dressed in yellow and had his head shaved and shiny like a well polished coconut, but unlike his friends he didn't follow his duties towards Buddha.

One day he was in a woman's house. When they heard her husband come back, the wife hid him in a sack and hung him from the rafters upside down.

"What's this bundle?" asked the husband, only noticing the golden colour through the mesh.

"This is a bell I have been asked to keep safe for the pagoda near-by."

So her husband, who loved the sound of bells, took out a mallet, because Chinese bells have no clapper, you know."

"Yes, I have seen them in the temple," nodded Minh.

"That's right; anyway, the husband gave an almighty blow to the side of the sack.

"Dong!" shouted the bonze.

"Ouch!" shouted Minh laughing while holding his head.

"Then another harder blow made him give out another, "Dong!" carried on his grandmother. "But the third even harder strike made him shout, "Help!"

"Ah, ah!" laughed Minh "I think the husband knew, don't you?"

"Most probably, I would have known by the first "dong"," smiled his grandmother.

"Please tell me another," pleaded Minh, who was so relaxed he wished the day would not end.

"Ok, but this is the last one. You must go home or your mother will be wondering where you are.

. . . When the king of heaven had created all beings, that were the people of Earth, he began to fear there might be some imperfections in his work. So he made it known to all the animals that he was ready to listen to their complaints and that he would attend to those which seemed justified. The animals crowded around his throne, for they all had something to say. Last of all came the crane, the hare and the mosquito.

The first complained that his feet were too delicate and out of proportion compared to the size of his body.

The king of heaven said to him, "then try to break them and when you have succeeded, come to me again and I will give you stronger ones."

"That's right," interrupted Minh. "You can see the crane when he alights, either on the water or on the ground, stamping his feet, trying to break them!"

"The hare then came and protested about his mouth, which seemed to him to be too small.

The king of heaven replied, "Well that is easy to remedy, I will make a slit to widen it."

"And this is why the hare has a slit in his mouth!" shouted Minh as if discovering something new.

"Yes, and do you know what it is called?

"No, what is it called?"

"We call it a "hare's lip," his grandma pointed out, mimicking the cut on her upper-lip.

What happened to the mosquito?" enquired Minh.

"Well, last of all came the evil mosquito. "You have made my sting too thin," he said, "it is not strong enough to stick through the skin of men and animals, so I can drink their blood whenever I am thirsty."

Then the king of heaven, exasperated by all these futile complaints said to him crossly, "I suppose you are right too, I will make sure that from now on you get help when you stick your sting in."

The mosquito went away happy and proceeded to find out if his wish had been granted. He began to sting man and beast wherever he went.

The promised help came . . . in the form of an unexpected slap from a hand, then a tail that finally crushed him."

"Good! I hate mosquitoes! Thanks for the stories," shouted Minh as one of the farmhands who had just come up the path, scooped him up in his arms.

"They are looking for him at the house," the man explained while bowing deeply towards the old woman.

"Good bye grandma!" Minh shouted as they started off towards his father's house. He could still see her on her step waving when he stated, "Father said I could have the day off. I'm not in trouble, am I?"

The man shook his head, just concentrating his strength in his muscle-bound arms. Minh had noticed him before lifting the wood with such ease that you would have thought each timber was made of cardboard. When he had told his father that he would love to be as strong, the reply had been that in battle physical strength was not as important as cunning.

He had noticed that his father statement had been right on several occasions. He thought about his judo lessons for example, where you didn't have to be big to put an opponent on the floor, even if he looked stronger than you.

When they reached the main house, he found his parents looking worried.

"What's happening, father?"

"Your Grandmother is not well. The doctor has just been to tell us that she is getting very frail. You mustn't bother her too much."

"But she was ok this morning! She told me lots of stories," smiled Minh.

"I know, she is a very strong minded woman and she does not want to slow down. When you get as old as she is you must take it easy, you can't do as much as before."

Minh hobbled to his mother who was very quiet and nuzzled her robes. Her hand rested on his head to soothe the worry that had invaded him. He pictured his Gran's slow movements and remembered that sometimes she had needed his help to steady herself.

5. Gongs and fireworks

One evening grandmother asked for her favourite meal. After eating from all the different dishes that Suu had brought to her on the usual tortoise shell tray, she said goodnight and went to bed. The next morning she had passed away in her sleep. It had been as if she knew it was her time. Minh was inconsolable. The house filled with people. Family were visiting from all different counties.

"Why are all these people coming now when we want to be on our own to think," Minh said to his mother, wiping the tears off his face.

"Because it is the custom, Minh. When someone dies you have to prepare a big meal for all that person's friend and family. It is a way for everyone to say farewell. We can then all remember that person together. Some might remember something and others may remember different things about them, and it feels good to remember all the good time we had together."

"But I am sad! I would prefer to be left alone so I could cry without anyone seeing."

"It is not bad to cry, Minh. You cry if you want to, if it makes you feel better. Everybody will understand and I'm sure they want to cry too. Go and put some incense in front of the ancestor's shrine it will make you feel closer to grandma."

Minh walked away towards the altar where each grandparent was represented by a flat polished stone. He picked up a few incense sticks and lit the end tip. A sweet warm smell invaded the room as the ribbons of smoke started their journey towards the heavens.

The funeral celebrations lasted three months. On the day of the burial, the procession walked to the edge of the family grounds. Minh noticed a glass full of water resting on the coffin.

"What is that?" he asked his mother puzzled.

"The pallbearers will be paid depending on how slow they carry the coffin to its final resting place," explained Suu. "Your father will see if they were careful by the amount of water there is left in the glass.

As they walked slowly towards the field where his grandmother would finally rest with the grandfather he had not known, Minh took in the eerie surroundings.

The tomb was protected by a small roof with upturned corners leaning on four pillars. Near it were other tombs of different members of the family. Surrounding all these, a small wall marked the limits of this sacred ground. The entrance to the ground was guarded by a stone where Chinese characters in bright colours warded off the evil spirits. In the fields further on, cattle were quietly grazing the thin dry grass. All seemed frozen under an unearthly shroud and Minh wondered if the red and gold dragons carved into the pillar next to him would suddenly come to life and take him away into the mist to some sinister place below.

That funeral and the Tet, Chinese New Year, were the two main celebrations Minh could not forget that year. New Year was a celebration which involved family and community togetherness and it lasted for a few days.

On the first day of Tet, Minh had noticed that the usually immaculate kitchen floor had been left upswept and asked his mother about it.

"This comes from a Chinese legend," she explained. "It is about a young housewife who lived in Heaven. Her duty was to cook the celestial meals, but she was extremely greedy and always ate loads from each dish to taste them. One day the Master of the Universe, in a rage exiled her to Earth and changed her into a broom. In future she would only pick up rubbish instead of the delicacies of Heaven."

"That was a bit harsh!" exclaimed Minh, "maybe she was hungry!"

"Well, she thought it was a bit unfair too and sent a prayer explaining that she worked all the time without a day's rest, and Heaven took pity on her and granted her a day off work on every New Year's day."

"Wah! Big deal! One day in a whole three hundred and sixty five!" shouted Minh.

"Anyway, that is why we do not use the broom on the first Tet day. The Kitchen God is keeping an eye on you, Minh," added Suu. "Have you been a good boy?"

"Yes, I have! What would happen if I had been a bad boy, mum?" said Minh, a little bit apprehensive after hearing the story of the kitchen maid.

"The Kitchen God watches over every home and at New Year reports to the Emperor of Heaven on each person's behaviour during the past twelve months."

"Would something terrible happen to someone who had not behaved?" whispered Minh.

Suu smiled but didn't answer. She just winked as she walked off to supervise the preparation of the dishes for the great meal. Flowers were on display everywhere. Minh waited in anticipation for the gifts wrapped in red tissue paper, that family and friends would dish out to all the children as they always did every year. He thought of a happy story that his grandmother had told him, how all the different names for each year came to be. He longed to hear her voice and imagined being in her room amid the silk cushions . . . her voice started singing in his head as he walked slowly towards the yard.

"Long ago in China . . ." Minh started recounting to himself. Suddenly he noticed his younger brother Tuy playing in the dust with a stick.

"What are you doing?"

"A rat just ran into these bushes!"

"Leave it alone! Come here I'll tell you one of Grandma's stories," he said as he dragged his younger brother by his sleeve until they reached the stone walls of the well. Tuy was a very quiet boy. He was six years younger than him and was easily led by his elders. Tuy sat down leaning against the stones and looked up at his brother. "It was decided that the years should be named after the animals that lived in the country, but the animals could not decide who should be first. They started arguing and woke up the gods. So the gods decided that they should compete in a swimming race across the river. The years would then be named in order that the animals would arrive on the other side. All the animals dived in and almost from the start the Ox took the lead, but just as it looked as if it were going to win, the Rat jumped on his back, then on his nose and finally on the river bank. The Rat had won through his cleverness, then came the Ox, the Tiger, the Rabbit, the Dragon, the Snake, the Horse, the Sheep" . . . Minh carried on, counting on his fingers . . . "the Monkey, the Rooster, the Dog and the Pig. "Dragon, that's a good idea," exclaimed Minh "where is my kite?"

Minh ran to the main house followed by his brother and soon came out with the colourful toy.

It had a caterpillar's body and a dragon's head. It soon danced in the sky like a magical sea serpent. Minh's hands were trembling as the force of the wind tugged on the strings.

"Everything seems to be done in a rush today," he said, more to himself than to Tuy who, his eyes towards the sky, was jumping around with delight.

It felt more peaceful outdoors together with nature. He noticed the clouds forming like a crowd of animals, all coming to greet him and his dragon and he laughed as he pointed towards them.

The day ended in fire works and lit up paper lanterns festooned the wavy path to the main house. It was an explosion of light from all the different villages in the district and the children who had come to share the festivities with Minh and his family enjoyed a carefree holiday.

Minh got up one morning as bright as a button. The sun was at its highest and it promised to be a marvellous thirteenth birthday.

"Good morning father!"

"Good morning son. Would you go to the cornfield for me?"

Minh was a little bit disappointed that nothing had been mentioned about his special day.

"Of course father, what do you want me to do there?"

"Check that the monkeys aren't doing too much damage. You know what they are like when the corn is starting to come out."

Minh nodded and went to the outbuilding to fetch a pike. Then he set on his way towards the golden fields. His step was light and he had a joyous song in his head.

As he approached one of the enclosures, he suddenly heard a noise. Frozen with fear, but also nagged by curiosity, he slowly moved some of the long reeds that blocked his view. "The Hungry Spirits from the other world have come for offerings, and I have no food for them!" he thought above the loud banging of his heart.

Suddenly he came face to face with a stag, standing there, proud and gigantic, his dark eyes looking like two ebony beads.

Minh was standing there in a trance, not daring to move a muscle. Then quick as a flash the animal turned and ran.

Minh woke from his dream-like trance and ran back towards the house.

"Father, father!" he shouted

"Your father had to go on business," said one of the hands. "What's the matter, anything wrong with the corn?"

"No, no," panted Minh trying to get his breath, "it's a deer, over there in that field. It's gone towards the river."

The man grabbed a horn and blew a long note. Everybody appeared from all over the compound. The dogs were brought and the spears were fetched.

Minh walked in front of the long procession of noisy men to show them where he had seen the animal. Nearing the field they suddenly became mute and their steps lightened. Minh pointed towards the river, which whispers could be heard above the rustling of the tall grass. Everyone took a strategic place to make sure the deer would not escape them.

"Help!" Minh shouted suddenly, "he is here in front of me!"

Spears came flying past and stuck to the creature's neck. He was brought down and put out of its misery. Minh felt saddened by this spectacle but knew that, that was their way of life. The animals of the forest gave them meat, skins and medicine from their bones. It was ok killing for what they needed. What was wrong was to kill for the sake of killing. That evening the meat would be rolled into the fire to be cleaned and shared around.

Minh brought home the largest share for having spotted the deer.

The next morning, Hao allowed Minh to go on the tiger-hunt. "A belated birthday present," he said to his son, who was so exited he started jumping up and down on the spot.

As they neared the forest, the dogs were barking with excitement too. Nets were laid on the outskirts along the tree line and their canine friends were let lose. Following their barks and making a lot of noise with their horn and gong the men marched with a steady pace towards the forest.

"Why all the noise!" Minh asked his father. "Wouldn't it be better if we were quiet to surprise the tiger?"

"We must try to disorientate the big cat. He knows we are here, and he is very cunning. If there is a lot of noise he will get a bit panicky and run towards us. Then we will catch him in our net. Watch for any claw marks on the bark of the trees."

"I suppose that's how he keeps his claws sharp?" murmured Minh getting concerned.

"That's his way of marking his territory."

The barking got fainter in the depth of the foliage. Suddenly the dogs came back running around towards them in circles, as if warning them of an imminent danger. The party started walking even more gingerly in the undergrowth. Minh copied his father trying not to make too much noise as he walked on the leaves scattered on the ground under his feet.

He held his breath at every noise, studying the trees above them and the bushes around them.

As if by magic, the king of the forest suddenly appeared in front of them, proud and arrogant, staring with his yellow eyes full of hatred. A battle of wills had begun. The dogs were growling, the men were teasing the animal with their spears in front of them, keeping a safe distance and at the same time knowing that if they showed fear the animal would pounce and attack with its sharp talons. His roar filled the forest. Slowly their prey was lured into a retreat towards the nets waiting behind the trees.

Time nearly came to a standstill. The beng-la started its monologue again.

As if hypnotised, the animal gave up the battle, turned and ran into the ropy mesh. The struggle was short as each spear brought him closer to its death.

"Son, do you know that there are no two tigers with the same markings?" said Hao as they were walking back with their trophy.

"But they all look the same!"

"Well, if you look closely they are not and apparently nor are their paw prints."

"They are like us then, different finger prints!"

"He was probably after the deer you caught yesterday. That would have been a good meal for him, but he eats smaller animals too."

"What other animals?"

"Tortoises, even frogs if that's all there is."

"How old do you think this one is father?"

"Maybe fifteen, they can live eighteen years, but fifteen is quite old. Usually they run away from you unless they feel threatened, or if they are too old to catch a prey. That's why you should not turn your back on one, if he attacks, he will attack your back."

Minh enjoyed these long talks with his father. Often, Hao was too busy to spend time with his children and left that job to his wife, although he knew it was important for the boys to know these things, so they could in turn tell their children and carry on the family customs. He knew how precarious their way of doing things had become in the regime of the foreigners.

6. Tears of anger

Minh was sitting in his favourite tree, the one closer to the main house, from where he could see a lot of the compound. He could see his favourite part of the garden where the larches, set near a pond, were waving in the warm breeze. Soft mosses edged small rocks surrounding the water where golden carp, spotted with red and black, waited with impatience for someone to throw in a handful of rice. From time to time their heads would come out on the surface, mouths wide open, forming like a necklace that seemed to sip the clear liquid. Sometimes one would jump in an impatient leap, splashing the thirsty ground and making the stones glisten in the sun.

Minh was carving a piece of wood with his pen-knife and was quite pleased with the way the eye of his dragon was turning out.

Suddenly, voices interrupted his concentration. His father, Thao and some of his friends had come into view from behind the building. They were gesticulating and speaking loudly.

"The French Headquarters in Hue has been stormed by the Revolutionaries," said Thao, his elder brother.

"Yes, someone tried to hoist our flag on their roof," laughed one of the men.

"Good for them!" agreed Hao.

"Two men were shot though," replied Thao.

"That won't stop them from trying again."

"The missionaries are charging heavy taxes again. People are really getting fed up."

"They are nothing but thieves hiding under their religious robes!"

43

"As soon as we get rid of some of them, more seem to reappear."

The group of men all dressed in long silky robes seemed to be talking in a very agitated way and were hardly giving time for each other to respond.

"They preach human kindness, but are more interested in filling their pockets!"

"Well, if you don't agree with the French you know you could end up in their prisons. We've got to be vigilant" said Hao trying to pacify his friends.

"Even our Emperor seems to work with the enemy!"

"That's right, Bao Dai and the Empress Nam Phung work hand in hand with those devils, Pasquier, Decoux and D'argenlieu!"

Although Minh didn't quite understand what was going on, he recognised his father's voice and knew he was in a really bad mood.

"No back-bone! All this is affecting the whole country now and we must do something about it."

Suddenly still hanging onto his branch, Minh heard some commotion near the gate. His mother was shouting at a group of French soldiers who had entered the compound unannounced. They stormed the group of men and grabbed his father, dragging him by his hair. It had fallen from its usually neat bun onto his shoulders. Minh's heart started to pound. He hoped his shape had merged into the foliage and that no-one would notice him. Hao's friends started shouting and waving their arms running around like mad men, but the soldiers carried on marching through the yard as if they didn't see or hear any of it.

As the foreigners disappeared past the main entrance Minh slid to the bottom of his perch. His mother, distraught, had gone inside with his brothers and sisters.

Keeping a safe distance he managed to follow the group of men to a stone building in a neighbouring village.

As he peered over the wall he noticed that his father had been hung by his hair. He was appalled. How these strangers could dare do this to his father, he did not know! This was beyond his comprehension.

The gaolers kept asking questions upon questions in their language. Then a Vietnamese looking man dressed in a blue overall translated in a shaky raucous voice.

"Who is in charge?"

The shouting was very unnerving. It seemed to Minh that they didn't even leave time in between each question for an answer. Their demands merged into one long, noisy sentence, which was incomprehensible. Then at last Minh just heard: "Names! Names!"

"Ok, I agree, I am anti-colonialist, because I love my country. You tell me that I instigate fights against you, but I am old and as you can see I have no weapon in my hand. How could I be fighting against you?"

Next to Hao, a woman who had been captured that day was not saying a word. She was just sitting on a low stool in a heap and she looked half asleep. Her hair was covering her face in a tangled matted mess and her dress was so torn that Minh could see her skinny legs were marbled with bruises.

Minh ran back to his house as fast as he could. He could not wait to tell his mother what he had witnessed. He hoped she would have a solution to the trouble they were now facing.

"Minh," she said, after he had told her all the details of the terrible ordeal, "go to Hue, you are very bright and maybe you can persuade the governor to let your father go. I know it won't be the same person as last month, which is a pity because your father knew him, but you can try your best."

"Maybe I could find father's friend . . ." started Minh hopeful.
"No, the French are careful not to leave the same people too
long in one place because people get to know each other.
They would make friends and that wouldn't do," said his
mother sarcastically.

Minh went on his way with a note for the foreign governor,
and a bag full of money. His mother had told him that maybe
money would be more powerful than words. It usually was.
As he arrived, he was told to kneel and wait. The bag and
the note were taken away from him. A tall man with his
hairy chest hanging out of his shirt appeared after a few
minutes, holding the paper that his soldier had passed on.
"This will cost you!" he smiled, but Minh noticed that his
eyes did not smile.
Minh didn't dare look up. He waited for an explanation.
What did the man mean? Was he going to be flogged for
having dared bring the note?
"I hope your father is rich, I want enough to be able to
retire from this god forsaken place," he added this time in
a sullen voice.
"Yes, my father is very rich!" exclaimed Minh, "I can bring
you more if you want tomorrow. Just let him go."
"It will be done when I see the money on the table," the
man stated as he turned away. Then he disappeared into
the building.
Minh stood up wondering if that meant he was dismissed.
Nobody seemed to pay any attention to him now. He crept
outside and ran as fast as he could.

As he arrived within sight of the house, he noticed his
mother peering towards the horizon. Minh started waving

vehemently. His legs ached but he did not stop running until he was next to her and collapsed at her feet.

In between breaths he reported what the foreigner had told him. As soon as he had finished, Suu went into the house. She managed to find more jewellery and raided the savings. Two trusted men were told to get to Hue with the parcel straight away.

That evening Hao was back.

"I'm cutting my plait!" he declared to Suu.

Suu cried gently as she imagined what he had gone through.

"Don't worry, I think they will leave us alone now. I can cause more trouble from inside their prisons than if they leave me with my family."

"I hope they do, I really do!" she whimpered. "We need you here."

"If something happens to me Thao will be in charge. Don't worry."

But that statement did not pacify her.

On the 14th of July Minh asked if he could go to town. The French were celebrating and he was curious.

"You be careful," whispered his mother. "Keep yourself to yourself and don't be back too late or your father won't be pleased."

"Please can I come?" pleaded Tuy.

"No, it's too dangerous!" frowned Minh.

"Please mum?"

"Minh, take your brother with you, and look after him. It is better not to be on your own anyway."

"But mum, what could Tuy do if we run into trouble!" exclaimed Minh.

"Go on, you'll be all right. Tuy doesn't have many opportunities to go to town."
"Come on then!" sighed Minh to his young brother.

In town the crowds were shouting and laughing. Foreigners and natives seemed to forget their differences eager to spend some good times away from their problems. Minh and Tuy squeezed through the human magma and ended up facing a circle of muddy ground. In the middle, a pole stood towards the sky, thicker at the top than at the bottom. A bag was tied at the top and Minh could see it was bulging. A peasant was trying to climb the pole jeered on by the screaming crowd, but the pole was covered in grease and his task seemed impossible. As expected he would slide back down in the mud where a wild pig was waiting to trample him savagely.

Minh grabbed his brother's sleeve and walked away disgusted. They came to another corner of the square and noticed two blind men and a boar locked into an enclosure.

"The aim of the game," a scruffy looking man was explaining, "is to try and grab the pig and tie him up to that post. Watch out, he bites!" the man laughed. It was a loud greasy laugh that seemed to fill the air like thunder.

Minh knew that it would be more or less impossible for the two beggars to do this. The wild animal, frightened by the surrounding noise, was grunting its anger and rushing towards the poor creatures cowering in a corner, arms stretched as if this would protect them from their imminent death.

Minh suddenly realised how his father was right in fighting against these foreigners who were bringing such disorder into their quiet villages.

Both brothers walked home and Minh was disappointed that he could not have stopped the men in the square. What could he have done on his own? Maybe if his friends had been with him . . .

That night he lay there immobile, stuck in the same position, limp like a rag doll. His limbs ached.

"Minh, are you awake?"

"I am now, Tuy! What do you want?"

"Why did those people put the blind men with the pig? They couldn't see when the pig was coming near them!"

"That's just it, silly. They thought it was funny to see them struggle."

"That's very unkind, isn't it?"

"Yes. Go to sleep will you!"

"One day teacher said that a blind man can sometimes see further than you and me though!"

"He meant that his experiences and his wisdom give him the knowledge rather than his eyes. Can I go to sleep now?"

Soon, ghosts of soldiers with whips were shouting and gesticulating in front of him. After what seemed an eternity, his mother's melodious voice poured through the partitioned wall and soothed away his aching head.

My sister of Asian Nights,
I delight in your beauty.
Your cheeks are like the flowers from the peach tree,
Your tunic is of light satin.
I breathe your intoxicating perfume.
Your hair is of blue silk,
Your carmine lips open on tiny silver teeth.
My friend, my sister, my child,
Give me your hand so my heart can sleep,
Give me your hand so I will be saved.

PART TWO

7. Change of ID

One morning in November 1939 Minh found his parents very agitated. As he approached the door he could hear their voices punctuated by the crystalline sound of the water spurting out of the guilt dragon laying in a nonchalant pose in the middle of the fountain.

"Bao Dai has signed the authorisation!" his father was saying shaking his head.

"All our teenagers!" his mother managed to articulate in disbelief.

"All twenty year olds, twenty five thousand of them will be enrolled by the end of the week."

"They will ship them over?"

"You know the French are at war, and they need to boost their army."

"But that means . . . Thao . . . ?"

"Yes, he knows that they will turn up one day for him. Quite soon I suppose." Hao was rubbing the lines that had, over the last couple of years, begun to appear on his brow.

Minh thought his father looked older today than he ever had. His slightly stooped silhouette was forming like a Japanese shadow on the bright square opening of the window.

His mother looked like a heap at his feet and from time to time she was dabbing her eyes with the corner of her sleeve.

Minh was fifteen, nearly a man, but not quite. He still was governed by impulses, which made him embark on what he thought were mysterious adventures.

They didn't have to wait long, by next morning, a French sergeant came to talk to his father. Minh recognised the insignia on his collar, which always seemed to go together with an abrupt tone of voice.

"We are looking for your eldest son! Where is he?" the soldier ordered.

"I thought he was with you," bowed Hao, with a steady voice. Minh thought that, knowing Thao, he was probably giving the French the run around. That was why his father looked at ease in front of the foreigner. He smiled at the thought that Thao was probably in the forest by now with some of his friends and no way would they be able to locate them. The forest was like a second home to him.

"If he is not back in three days," shouted the sergeant, "you will be taken away. So you better tell him to get down from your loft pronto!"

Minh's mind was racing. Thao was not in the loft, he was sure of that. In fact he hadn't seen him for a few days now. If Thao had known what trouble his actions were beginning to create for his parents, he probably would be here now.

Minh didn't know his brother very well. Thao's temperament was rather sombre and he preferred writing and meddling in politics with his father rather than playing in the fields with his brothers and his friends. Suu had explained to her second son that Politics and Philosophy were a very popular topic for men in their family, and that when he was older he too would probably join them in the main house for long discussions. That is why he had to pay attention in school, to become "learned like his father and his older brother". Minh was not convinced though. He still thought that catching the tiger or running after the monkeys through the corn fields were more exciting past-times.

Three days later the foreign sergeant was back as promised. Thao was still missing.

"How much do you want?" enquired Hao still sure of himself.

"It is not money we need, but arms to carry our guns!" shouted the soldier irritated. The veins on his neck were now forming ridges like the plough would in the dirt. "Nguyen Van Thao! That's what's written on my paper!" he spat out. Suddenly looking at Minh, he beckoned him waiving a fat index finger in the humid afternoon air.

"No!" shouted Hao, running towards his boy to protect him with his body "You've got it wrong, this is our second son. He is only fifteen! This is not Thao!"

But the man was not listening anymore and started pushing Minh in front of him.

Suu and Minh's sisters, who had come out of the house by now, were crying, a soft gentle lament which rose towards a suddenly cloudy sky.

"Never mind father. I'll go instead of Thao if this prevents you from going into that dreadful jail again."

"It will be for three years Minh!" said Hao shaking Minh's arm as if to wake him up from a nightmare.

The sergeant had stopped pushing and was writing on his piece of paper not paying attention to the family standing there in front of him. Another family he was tearing apart.

"It will go quickly I'm sure. It will be an adventure! Think of all the things I will be able to talk to you about when I get back. I'm going on the other side of the world!" exclaimed Minh smiling.

"Yes, our land has sharp nails to drag back whoever touches her. You will be back, for no-one could keep away from her!" declared Hao to his son, looking deep into his eyes as if to make sure that what he was hoping for would become reality.

"I was talking to Truong only yesterday morning, lots of boys from the village have already gone. His brother has gone," added Minh. "Stop worrying!"

The sergeant was getting impatient now, huffing and puffing as Suu got a bag ready and gathered the whole family. The sun was already setting behind the trees creating a pink water-colour where the vegetation appeared like shadowy hands reaching out from the earth.
"Look after yourself!" cried Suu, "you'll soon be back!" she said trying to convince herself.
Everyone, blurry eyed, pushed their pictures into his pockets as if to give him a little bit of themselves. They wanted to give him some well needed strength.

Minh had changed identity. He was now Thao. He was not fifteen anymore but twenty-one. He was a man! He was excited.
Minh waved his good-byes. He didn't know that this was the last time he would ever see them again, but felt a mixture of elation and apprehension mounting in his heart.
On his army papers was written: Nguyễn Văn Thảo, Number ZAD 260, Born in Cu Nam in 1918, District of Hoan Phuc Huyen of Bo Track. Quang Binh province. Annam. Bachelor. Farmer. Son of Nguyen Van Hao and Nguyen Thi Suu. VOLUNTEER.

He was drafted on the 17th of January 1940 in Dong Hoi, the next town South of his village. It was the dawn of the year of the Dragon. The first six months, he was posted in Saigon, where every day he had to exercise with his companions in a dusty yard.

They were given boots, shirts, jackets and a set of aluminium canteens, which had to be kept spotless. All their belongings were kept in a heavy duty canvas back-pack, which they had to drag around on every manoeuvre.

Minh was also proud of his beret and posed for several pictures with his friends, hoping to be able to post them to his family before he left the country.

No one questioned his small stature as, on the whole, all his friends in arms were quite small. The sergeant there seemed to like him and picked him to be his Corporal. He was in charge of secretarial duties which suited him fine. His resourcefulness made him popular with his comrades as well as with the foreign soldiers. He felt he was going to have a good time for a few years, then come back full of stories to tell.

It was the 20th of February when they were told that a group of them would be leaving Saigon for Marseilles on the war-ship Forbin. On their papers they noticed these words: "Colonial Manual Workers".

"That is it!" shouted Minh to the soldier next to him. "We are off!"

Minh looked around him at all the faces. Some he knew well from the village others he recognised as coming from Southern provinces. Some had smiling faces at the prospect of a trip to a country full of riches and promises, others were tearful at leaving what they were accustomed to behind.

"Truong!"

"Minh! What luck! Tai is here too."

The three friends embraced in the middle of the crowded room under the surprised look of their comrades.

Suddenly, as he scanned around to see if there were more of their mutual friends assigned to their group, Minh noticed that some of the youngsters had blackened teeth.

He remembered asking his teacher about this before. The teacher had explained that this was a fashion in rural parts. Minh thought it very strange and decided he should ask the man himself.

"My black teeth," laughed the man, who looked older than the rest of them, "it's because I chewed betel, I have a digestive problem, but them over there, I think they did it because of fashion."

"Strange fashion!" exclaimed Minh. "Rather ugly!"

"Well everyone to his own," smiled the old man. "Of course you know how they do it? Not with betel."

"No? How?" inquired Minh.

"Well, you mix about three pints of hot water and half a cup of Saki, add some red hot iron, leave the mixture for three days and collect the scum."

"Huh!" interrupted Minh grimacing.

"Add some powdered gallnut," continued the man counting on his skinny fingers, "and some iron filings". Reheat and apply to the teeth with a brush."

"That's disgusting!" shouted Minh, beckoning one of his mates to tell him about what he had just learnt.

"People do extraordinary things for fashion sake," laughed the man showing off his brown mouth. His eyes were glistening with excitement at the reaction he had caused.

The crossing to Marseilles lasted forty days. Lots of Minh's comrades were ill and some even died. Minh started to think that this new adventure was not going to be as much fun as he had anticipated. Holding on to the rigging he tried his best not to lose his footing. He sat on his bag which contained the few precious things his father had put in at the last minute. He had already bartered some of them against some privileges for himself and his closest friends.

They were all used to opened spaces and finding themselves confined on this mountain of steel, on this non-stop roller-coaster, really did not agree with most of them.

They didn't arrive at their destination until the 3rd of April. Minh felt dizzy as his feet touched the foreign soil. The ground moved beneath him as if he had just drunk a gallon of wine. Most of them just felt sick and collapsed in a heap on the dock, their head in their hands and breathing deeply, trying to fight back the heaving that was taking over their bodies.

"Men of the 54th Regiment!" shouted the General emphatically, "France will win!"

As they followed their new chief to their compound, the walk helped them get a grip on their new surroundings.

The next morning, Minh was woken up by frantic voices. He could not fathom out what was going on as it was all in a different language.

"Truong, what's all the noise about?" he asked his companion.

"Apparently the Germans have gained on us and we've been told to grab our kit and run."

"We've only just arrived!" exclaimed Minh.

"I know, but if you value your life I'd advise you to hurry up, I think we've landed in a trap. The town was already taken," shouted his friend as he threw his bag on his shoulder and started running towards the ditch which was hemming the dusty road.

Minh did the same with his holdall and ran like a rabbit trying to keep up with his group. Along the ditch, then through the fields, he zigzagged like a hare on the run from a fox. After what seemed to be hours, out of breath, he stopped at the foot of a cherry tree. His boots were too big for him. They hadn't been able to find the right size for him. Most men were a seven or over and he was only a five. The boots had been rubbing all the while on his heels, which were now on fire. He decided to throw them away and bare foot started to climb the tree.

8. On the Run

Minh suddenly heard voices. From his perch he looked down onto two German soldiers. Their shiny helmets stared at him from below and their glare pained his eyes. The soldiers had stopped for a cigarette and the smoke was now invading his precarious hideout. Suddenly he lost his footing on one of the thin branches causing a shower of bark and foliage on the two heads beneath him.

"Kommen! Kommen!" the soldiers shouted, brandishing their arms at him.

Minh climbed down and grabbed his bag that was still laying there at the bottom of the tree. He wondered how they had not noticed it before, but maybe its dark greenish colour had blended somehow with the ground.

The two men now pushing him in front of them started in the direction of a village, which he could see in the valley, its small church towering above the houses like a protective parent.

When they arrived at the town-hall, the German commandant was waiting in the large door embrasure. The impressive stone surround made it look like a frame and the man's imposing figure towered above Minh.

Minh was not intimidated though and was just wondering if he would be allowed to eat. He hadn't eaten for days it seemed and his stomach was beginning to ache. He grimaced with pain and the foreigner thinking it was from fright started smiling with disdain.

"Where is your colonel? Your commandant?" he shouted.

Minh made some signs to the right then to the left. He rubbed his hands together to show that he didn't know and that, really, he didn't care. Then a small Asian man arrived. He was old and wrinkled, but Minh thought his face looked friendly. He repeated to him that he didn't know where his battalion was. He was lost and hungry. Luckily for him they seemed to believe him. He thought that maybe because he was so short compared to them, they thought he was not important. Not worth bothering with. They waved him away and the Asian man led him towards a building.

By the smell and the noise of pots and pans, he thought, this must be the kitchens.

Minh sat down at the wide wooden table. It was laden with dishes full of meat and bread. On the stove was an enormous pot where a stew was bubbling gently. Next to him a basket full of fruit beckoned. Minh grabbed a handful of apples, stuffed them in his bag and scampered through the opened door.

He didn't stop for ages. He ran along the cobbled streets, past the deserted shops, breathless but willing himself to carry on, pushed by an invisible force and by the rhythm of the rumble in his temples and in his chest. He finally reached the woods on the other side of the village and collapsed in a heap onto the cool grass.

"Minh!" whispered a voice from behind a bush.

"Who is it?" murmured Minh startled.

"Me," said a figure crawling from the undergrowth.

Minh recognised one of his comrades and smiled with relief. They shared the fruit and were soon met by more of their friends, one of the French sergeants and the radio engineer. They had all been roaming the countryside in the hope of finding a familiar face, and especially in the hope of finding their unit.

"Let's go!" said the sergeant. "We've got to try to regroup."

"The factory at Ripault has caught fire, sergeant. Intensive bombing from the German army, sir," reported the radio operator. "Apparently it has been burning for more than a week!"

"Not surprising," answered the officer taking his cap off and tearing at his epaulettes, "it was a powder factory."

"Sir?" questioned the soldier, "have we lost?"

"I think I have a better chance if I get rid of these, don't you? The Germans seem to be gaining on us and they don't take kindly to soldiers of a certain rank."

For fourteen days and fourteen nights Minh and his friends ran from field to field in the hope of finding the rest of their battalion. At night they would huddle together to keep warm. Sometimes farmers would leave some bread and wine in large dustbins on the edge of their fields. Other times as they passed in front of a house they would knock for food only to have the door slammed in their faces. After what seemed miles of aimless running and hiding in hedges, Minh declared to his friend:

"Let's get rid of our guns!"

"Are you mad! Without them we are dead!"

"On the contrary, I think we have a better chance without them. If we are spotted armed, their reaction will be to fire before we do."

"You are right," the group agreed.

"And anyway, what have we got against the Germans?" he added, emphasising the "we" while looking towards his Vietnamese friends.

The clinking of the guns soon stopped as they were dumped in the ditches. They resumed their walking with more ease. They came to a clearing. It looked like a mini meadow surrounded by tall trees. The grass was short like it had been mowed. Minh stared out towards the canopy. Across the lawn two men lay dead next to each other. Minh got closer. He noticed that one man's abdominal cavity was emptied around him, his remaining arm buried under his own gut.

The other seemed to be sleeping, but as he approached him, Minh noticed that half of his head was missing. Minh waved to his companions to slow down. Were they in a mine field? He studied the ground. His friends, suddenly understanding, did the same. On the other side of the row of trees was a path and they decided that it might be safer to take that option.

Walking along the straight but narrow road, they suddenly came face to face with two enemy motorcyclists.

"Halt!" said the first one.

"Where is your NCO?"

Minh waved his hands, as Tai who could speak a little French stated:

"We not know. Them run away!"

The armed soldiers waved them on and made them march what seemed like miles. Minh's limbs felt as if they didn't belong to him.

"AMBOISE, that's what the sign on the side of the road said," Minh told his friends as they were hurdled into the cathedral for the night. The building was cold and shadows were dancing on the walls. The flicker of a lonely candle was conjuring some lonely ghost. Minh tried to steal a few minutes of soothing rest.

Too soon a colonel came and the silence was broken by his shouts, which echoed across the voluptuous ceiling of the church. They were ordered to line up against the wall outside. Minh noticed that they had not been alone in their stony prison. Some Malagasy, Senegalese and Algerian soldiers were being pushed around too. These were in their underwear and looked dishevelled, haggard, dirty, as if they had been there for several months and hadn't seen daylight in all that time.

"This is our lot," thought Minh. "Our luck has run out!"
He sighed with resignation. He was so tired that he thought
a long peaceful rest would be really welcome.

The men in front of them started a long discussion, which
was incomprehensible to them. Suddenly they grabbed their
guns. Minh shut his eyes and dug his fingers into a fist. His
feet adhered to the ground like two suckers. He suddenly
thought that he should have shouted a bit more, answered
back, screamed and swore at them, and then they might
have seen that they too were humans. They had said "line
up!" and they had. He had stood there with his friends,
stony faced and impassive and the foreigners had not seen
them as humans but as lower creatures from the forest.

His family invaded his mind, waving at him with smiles on
their faces. They were waiving away the abrupt end to his
childhood.

Then the image was torn by a shattering noise exploding
in his head as the soldiers poured death over their pitiful
group. The bullets got to their destination like ravenous
jackals would have pounced on their prey.

Then it was absolute silence and darkness. Minh felt warm
and sticky. His body was drenched by a substance which
had indecently adhered to his clothes and hit him in the
face. He didn't dare look or make a sound, as if he might
wake the other people lying down around him.

He suddenly felt he had become part of the dust of life!
Why were people destroying each other and everything
around them instead of using their brain to create? Maybe
God was a practical joker and this was his big anti-creation
joke. Maybe man was not meant to understand it all.

The soul is much more fragile than the body. The human
capacity for pain is like the bamboo, far more flexible than
you'd expect. Minh started to pray Buddha that he should

allow him a crumb of his immense compassion to take the place of the anger which was now welling in his throat. His throat hurt and all those tears that he had been saving came out of their hiding place.

Suddenly there was movement next to him.

Minh's mother: Nguyễn Thị Sưu

Aunt Hue

Nguyễn Văn Minh 1940

Marie Louise 1945

9. Fighting Spirit

To Minh's surprise he and his friends were still alive. Each side of them the bodies of their fellow prisoners were scattered along the base of the wall like discarded rag-dolls. They were all crumpled up like withered flowers. Minh's mind was racing.

Death suddenly appeared to him in its obscene simplicity. In a single movement life had disappeared like the dew in the morning sun.

He looked at his friends. Two tears had appeared, imperceptible droplets hanging onto his gaze. Why had they been spared? He didn't dare move a muscle now, fearing that this would attract attention and make the soldiers change their mind. He could hear his heart pounding and was sure the man next to him could hear it too, maybe even see it through the layers of his soiled clothes. He thought maybe they would just be taken somewhere else and shot there. Why, he didn't know. Hundreds of questions were rushing in his head. He looked again around him. How could a man kill someone in cold blood, and someone who was not armed? Didn't this show some sort of cowardice? With collective assassinations you could hide behind the bullet of your neighbour, since no-one could be sure if his own gun was the one which had caused death.

"Kommen!" shouted one of the soldiers.

Minh woke from his trance but shut his eyes tight. He could not see the man moving, but the voice was insistent.

"Kommen! Kommen! Schnell!"

He tried to hum then counted to himself, but the words infiltrated his ears. Then he put his hands on the side of his head, but the sounds persistently crept past his fingers.

Like a robot Minh followed his comrades.

The group soon arrived at a large farm building and Minh noticed that the foreign soldiers started to relax. Their attitude towards them mellowed. Some other of their Vietnamese friends were already there, walking aimlessly in the yard. An old tractor stood against the stone wall of a stable, but there was no sign of animals or farmhands.

"Hello you lot!" Minh beckoned in disbelief, "what's going on?"

"They only want us to cook for them," one of his comrades answered, smiling.

"Yes, they keep asking us what sort of music we like, things like that," said another.

"They wanted me to teach them judo," piped in another.

"Very strange attitude, considering we are supposed to be their enemy," stated Minh.

"Yes, but don't forget that the Japanese are their allies, maybe they cannot understand the difference . . ." smiled one of the friends knowingly.

"Hum, ok, let's make the most of it. It might not last when their officers arrive."

They all agreed that the position they were in at that moment was more than a little bit precarious. It was a period in their lives when they could not predict what would happen. They certainly had no control over their future.

Sure enough the next day as soon as day broke they were woken up by the booming voice of a one-eyed German officer. He looked like somebody out of a cartoon. His round and short stature, circled by a wide leather belt made you think of a barrel and his complexion betrayed someone who was partial to alcohol.

"In 1917, I was prisoner in a French camp. We were left without food for eight days. It is your turn today," he spluttered as he waved his orders to his troop. Minh thought he looked like a Cyclops.

The youngsters were hurdled into a barbed wire compound and then left to fend for themselves.

After a week the Cyclops returned. Minh bent over in hunger pain could just about distinguish his shadow as he stood, his back to the sun.

"Man is an animal subject to cold and hunger, and whoever can hold him by these means can make himself his master!" the Cyclops declared with pride.

Minh felt anger rising in his throat and got up. With as loud a voice as he could muster he shouted back: "Can't you show some humanity! How big you are in front of poor retched figures!" he carried on waving towards his companions whose pallid faces betrayed their exhaustion.

Minh suddenly felt the pain of a blow to his stomach replace the pain of hunger. Then one more time . . . this time his face felt as if it had exploded.

Like a sack of potatoes he hit the ground. His mouth was pouring with blood. He spat out. His teeth lay in front of him in the red dust. His friend rushed to him and helped him to his feet. Stumbling at each step they went towards the edge of the compound where they sat leaning against the wire mesh.

"Wha apen?" Minh managed to mumble.

"One of them hit you with his bayonet and his gun-but broke your teeth."

"My stomach too!" Minh creased up in pain.

His fingers started to tremble as if they had an independent life of their own. His eyes widened by the vision of a nearing death. On what was left of his khaki jacket, which was worse for wear, a brownish stain had suddenly appeared.

To calm him, Truong took him in his arms and brought him back for a few seconds towards his childhood days.

Their heads were shaved and the next day they were ordered to stay in a squatting position. All hunchbacked the poor wretches crawled to get some food. Those who attempted to get up were hit on the head. By the time they got back to their corner the remnant of a thin gruel could be soaked up with a piece of dried bread.

"I hate this!" spat out Minh, "they are treating us worse than insects! We are no trouble after all, it's not even our war! Why did I ever leave my world of games and dreams!" he carried on to himself.

"Think about Zen." Whispered Truong, sitting near him with his eyes closed.

"Zen?"

"Didn't you listen to teacher? The Buddhist concept of nothingness."

"Ah, that . . ." Minh started to think. He began to ponder on the fact that even silence, if it was understood in contrast with sound, would miss the point of Zen. "I remember: The West has always had a tendency to admire the gargantuan."

"And the East the Lilliputian," piped in Truong, repeating the lesson parrot fashion.

"But it is of little importance so long as we worship God whether He be infinitely great or infinitely small," carried on Minh with his eyes closed. "Do you think that the Cyclops believes in God?"

"I don't know, he certainly doesn't act like he does!"

Minh felt really lucky to have devoted friends around him. He had become so weak from the loss of blood, but they had helped him recover from his wounds as best they could. There was a rusty pipe at one end of the compound and Truong, his brow showing the weight of his newly found responsibility, would go and soak a piece of his shirt to bring back the precious liquid to Minh who could not walk more than a few painful paces at a time. The cloth was rather grubby but they were past caring about such details. From time to time Minh would go into a sort of trance where he didn't know which of his actions or which of his thoughts were really his.

"We are not soldiers anymore," he declared one day to his friend, "we have been reduced to nothingness."

After several days, which seemed to merge into one, the one-eyed man decided to send Minh to hospital. Minh was worried about leaving Truong behind.

The two of them tapped each other, brushing each other's hands, to seal up a deal that didn't need to be put into words. Minh looked back as he was being carted away.

He didn't hear what Truong shouted, just noticed the young man's skinny right arm extended in a long wave like the branch of a weeping willow.

At the hospital, confusion reigned in the overcrowded rooms. Row after row of men without hope, lay there in a stupor, faces sullen with disappointment or shock, marked with suppressed anger and exhaustion. Doctors and nurses were trying their best to patch up the hurts of the world, rushing in and out of the rooms like demented clowns.

"You seem better in yourself Minh," smiled the nurse one morning.

Minh was surprised to hear his own language. Although the accent was not quite the same as back home, it felt like a bit of fresh air had suddenly seeped through the grubby walls of the ward.

"I've decided that what is happening to me must be because of some sin I've committed in some previous existence. I must need to expiate it," answered Minh

"I see," replied the nurse unconvinced. "Is it what you call karma? Well if it helps you to hold on, this is good."

The angel of mercy tucked the patient in and straightened his pillow. He noticed that she was not as young as she first appeared, although her hair was still jet black, tied back in a neat bun. Calm and gentleness oozed from her face and her hands were as white as lotus blossoms.

"I think that good and evil must necessarily alternate, so some good must be coming my way soon."

"This is very philosophical, young man," said the nurse obviously impressed. "That's the spirit. Keep your chin up "

"This is a Confucian concept. My father's religion."

He could almost say that he wasn't afraid anymore. His well known stubbornness would help him. He did not suffer from the panic he could see on some of his comrades' faces. He found comfort in his memories. He would survive this captivity by wrapping himself in them, as if they were an invisible armour.

He tried to forget what he had seen and felt. Whole towns destroyed, from which the inhabitants must have run for their lives, completely deserted. Cadavers of men and women and children too, had appeared scattered across streets, the only movement being ribbons of smoke climbing up from the few abandoned houses. The terrible smell of smoke mingling with the smell of death was still hanging on to his nostrils. "With memory comes knowledge and with knowledge comes pain," he decided.

He reached for his bag. He was grateful it had been brought to him after an anxious day and a half. After rummaging past the aluminium utensils and clothing, he grabbed a soiled envelope. In it were the photographs of his beloved family. How far away they seemed at that moment! How he longed for their embrace!

He remembered his mother saying to him, when he would not pose still for the shot to be taken, "a photograph says that you were happy and I wanted to catch that feeling. It says that you were so important to me that I put down everything to come and watch." How glad he was that he had these pictures with him now. He suddenly felt less alone, because as nature becomes green again and regenerates after a fire, man rebuilds slowly after turmoil.

10. A law onto themselves

A radio was announcing that the Germans were on one side of the river Loire and the French on the other.

Minh started thinking about escaping. He was already planning getting back home. He could already smell the agaves, the magnolias and the lotus and feel the caressing breeze, soft "as a young girl from Hue", his brother Thao used to say.

Finally, one warm evening, he had made up his mind.

"I'm off tonight!" Minh whispered to himself as his senses awakened to the strong smell and the noises of the hospital.

As darkness invaded the room and the flickering lights were extinguished one by one, Minh rolled out of bed. For a second he felt his side where the pad had been replaced every morning. He grabbed the photographs he had put under his pillow, collected the few souvenirs he still had from his father and pushed the rest of his belongings under the bed. He had to travel light if he wanted to be fast.

After throwing on shirt and pants, he crept out, past the head nurse's room and along the cold endless corridor.

From time to time a noise or a distant voice would stop him in his stride. Soon he found himself outside. He couldn't believe how easy it had been. Where were the guards? Maybe a call of nature, or a five minute lapse in their duties. It didn't matter, he was outside and started running along the walls, merging in the shadows, making himself invisible.

He suddenly came to the river and remembered the radio announcement. Finding some renewed strength he decided to swim. He was a good swimmer, "like a fish" his mother would say. The water was freezing and Minh thought for a moment that he would surely turn into a block of ice. His extremities felt as if they didn't belong to him anymore. He was thankful that he had the endurance of an Olympic swimmer, but each movement was tearing an involuntary cry out of his lungs and his small bag weighed him down as if he were carrying a piece of lead.

After what seemed a lifetime Minh reached the other side. He clawed at the bank with all his might. His soppy clothes were heavy and sticking to his chest, restraining his breathing.

When you are on the run, time does not exist anymore. From time to time he had to stop to sleep and then he would start his long march again usually at night. He would eat what he could pinch from shop windows. His observation skills were his weapon. His decisions were quick and sharp. There was no time for thinking at length. Sometimes he would sleep under a bridge with no other companions but the rats. His feet were getting sore but he didn't pay too much attention to the pain. He was not quite sure where he was going. He hoped deep down he would eventually meet a friendly face. His stomach would often burn with hunger but if he were lucky he could eat berries and wild mushrooms, which he had learnt in the past to recognise, or if he were unlucky he would resort to eating worms. His mind was only filled with the will of getting "there", wherever that was, as day and night joined up into a long unidentified oblivion.

He had to keep running as far away as he could from where the soldiers would by now have realised he had given them the slip. Under the cover of darkness he would run from field to field, past farm houses, and then as day broke he would find himself a hiding place to rest until dark again.

Ghosts from the past would come and torment him. Sometimes he would find himself tied by the wrists, dragged by a horse whose emaciated body was competing with his own. Other times he was locked into a damp room with no windows, but the stony walls covered in moss did not have the expected softness. The green blanket was full of spines and would wake him with a jerk.

From time to time a dog would invade the silence of the darkened streets. He was studying the shadows with the vigilance of a lamb detecting the smell of the lion. After wondering from street to street in the town he had just reached, Minh noted on both sides rows of houses which seemed deserted and decided to try one of the doors. He was hungry and the pain in his stomach would not let him wait any longer for an easier opportunity. As he slowly turned the handle, the door groaned like Aladdin's cave. Suddenly a force that was not his own opened it wide. The light of a candle stabbed him in the eyes. A hand grabbed him with the force of an iron vice and pulled him inside before shutting the locks as quickly as it had opened.

"Where am I?" asked Minh in a daze. He wanted to run but didn't have the strength anymore. His feet suddenly felt like lead.

"You are in Vaucluse, and this is my house!" exclaimed a man in his fifties. He was speaking slowly and using gestures. He had noted that the boy in front of him was not from the area and although he had a suspicious look on his face, Minh had a feeling all was ok.

The man had a beret slanted over one eye and was dressed in heavy duty linen trousers. A faded shirt was opened onto a thick neck and Minh could see that the man's skin was darker than any other French man he had met before.

"My name Minh, 54th Regiment," he ventured.

"Oh, one of us!" a voice suddenly called out.

Minh stepped back two paces. In front of him he suddenly noticed that they were not on their own. The flicker of the candle uncovered a long wooden table taking nearly all the space of a low ceiling room, and round it were half a dozen men sitting in front of wine and a plate of cheese. A man walked up from somewhere towards them out of the darkness and sat beside them at the table. His face suddenly flashed into existence as he lit up a cigarette. "You are hungry!" laughed the man holding the candle high, as he noticed Minh's widened eyes. "Sit down!" he barked in a baritone voice as he pushed him towards a straw chair.

The man was tall and as wide as a Norman wardrobe. His shadow added height to his giant appearance. His bald head was shining in the dim light, but he soon remedied that by pulling a dark woolly hat over it, still puffing away at the white stick in his mouth.

They started to talk amongst themselves in a murmur as Minh tucked into a slab of cheese. He hadn't had cheese often before. Only when his father had taken him to the French restaurant had he tried it gingerly. The consistency was weird, but creamy and today it felt extremely good in his dried-up mouth.

"I am Commandant Gallo" said the elderly man who had sat down next to him handing him his hand. "We've decided we can trust you. We are the Resistance. You understand? And as from today, so are you."

Minh nodded still munching on a piece of bread.

"We know where the Germans have their ammunitions and we are planning to blow it up. Of course we have to wait for the right moment. You are coming with us when the time comes, probably tomorrow night if the coast is clear."

"Why not tonight?" answered Minh. "The streets are deserted."
"Are you sure?"
Everyone looked up from the table.
"Yes, I crossed river, walked about all day . . . no one about because of the rain."
"God, look at you, you are soaked!" The commandant looked at him as if he had only just set eyes on him, "here put this on," he added as he rummaged in the corner of the room in a pile of what looked like a mound of papers, baskets full of bottles and old faded clothes. He handed over a shirt and a pair of trousers, which seemed miles too big for Minh who only looked like a young boy compared to these strong looking men.

After Minh got changed and tore off at least six inches of the trouser legs, they decided that maybe tonight would be a good time. The table was cleared and a map of the town and its surrounding areas was spread over the wooden planks. Minh left the men to their discussions and as he sat on the floor in the corner of the room he decided that he had been quite lucky to have finally found some friends.

He woke up from his doze to the sound of a murmured refrain. His new comrades were standing around the table, a glass in their hand, suppressing their voices as they chanted:

"Friend, can you hear the dark flight of the black bird on the plains!
Friend, can you hear the dull cries of the land in chains!
Eh, followers, workers, artisans, get ready!
This evening, the enemy will know the price of blood and tears!
Come out of the mines; get down from the hills,
Comrades!"

"A job well done," stated their leader, as he clicked the glass held next to his.

"You do job?" asked Minh "You come back!"

"Yes, and a great success it was. They haven't got any ammunition in our neck of the wood anymore!" smiled the man, nodding to his comrades.

They all nodded back, grunting their agreement.

"You were sleeping like a baby; we didn't want to wake you. There'll be other times don't you worry!"

Minh felt something under his leg. It was a wallet. As he brandished it above his head, the commandant rushed towards it.

"I've been looking for that all day! I've got all my family photos in it. Come on Paul!" and he grabbed Minh by the arm. "Let me show you the family."

"My name Minh!" Minh protested.

"Well, to me you are Paul. You remind me of a Paul," the man said, as he started rummaging in the leather pouch for the pictures he wanted to show.

Minh knew that names didn't matter anyway in these circumstances, hadn't he already changed his name?

After that day, the leader of the group started coming to the part of the house, which had been allocated to him. It was just a corner where a metal framed bed stood and a set of draws where he could put the few things he still possessed. They would sometimes settle down for a chat in the evening. Commandant Gallo was curious about the shrine that Minh had built on the wooden floor. It was made of small pieces of wood standing on the ground in an L shape with some Chinese writing on the vertical bits. In front of it Minh had put the few pictures his family had given to him when he had left that fateful day. A couple of incense sticks stuck in tiny holes were sending to the sky a ribbon of fragranced prayers.

"We honour ancestors," explained Minh to his new friend. "Have to maintain a balance between two worlds."

"What do you mean, "two worlds"?"

"The world of shadows and the world of light," said Minh surprised that someone didn't know about this.

"Why should you have to maintain a balance, when you are dead, isn't it the end?" exclaimed the incredulous man laughing.

"Lost ghosts of the dead may invade living world! Caring for ancestors is very important," said Minh, surprised that such a kind man did not seem to know Confucius wisdom.

"You are right in the fact that we should not forget our roots, and in so doing our ancestors," murmured the soldier, "if more did this, we would live in a better world, I'm sure."

"This, Confucius way," repeated Minh, nodding his head.

"Is that like Buddhism?"

"Buddhism comes from China. Buddhism is method where by power of meditation human beings can free themselves from all pain and from perpetual rebirth, so it is not quite same as Confucianism."

"I've never heard of Confucia-er-thingy, is that Vietnam's religion then?"

"Vietnam received lot of religious influences in past, but it is Confucianism that has shaped and formed Vietnam society."

"Isn't it a feudal structure over there, with peasants and lords?" Minh laughed at the sketchy explanation. "I suppose you right. Life in my country is mostly agricultural. It was from agricultural life that human ideal was conceived. The population from 4th century was intellectualised slow, slow."

"What do you mean "human ideal"?" interrupted the man.
"Confucian morality not founded on divine revelation but built on realities. It is a philosophy which is inclined to take form of reflexion and advice. Never uses abstract."

"That sounds good to me! Something built on realities must be more understandable and so much more approachable," declared Commandant Gallo. "You may have a convert here," he added patting Minh on the back.

"Well, when you are convinced about idea, you are always tempted to attract your friends into embracing it too," smiled Minh.

He was glad he had found this man at a time when he needed friendship more than at any other time.

"The Americans have arrived in Normandy, so maybe we'll be rid of the Germans here in the South soon," said the Commandant as he got up to leave him. "Let's get some sleep now!"

Minh lay on his bed. Imperceptibly, misery and solitude slowly invaded his mind, behind his shut eyes. Slowly the trees abandoned their lush foliage to leave the space to more and more spinier plants, stunted, as if the fight against dryness had been a war with no rules. Villages were more and more spaced out until there were only a few isolated huts. Minh suddenly started running, nearly flying! He was escaping from an invisible force which seemed to be trying to suck him into a time warp.

11. No Turning Back

It was 1945 and Minh had rejoined the regular army. He was Warrant Officer in the 31st Company during the German occupation.

His colonel had called the battalion officers for a meeting that morning.

Minh came down from the room he had been allocated in one of the numerous farm dotted around the countryside, to a putrid smell coming from the kitchen.

"What is that!" he exclaimed, as he pushed the door open.

In front of him, on the table were hundreds of little round wooden boxes, which a rather large woman was trying to stuff into a chest.

"Camembert!" she explained with a broad smile and a strong German accent. "Delicious, typical Norman cheese. They have been sent to feed you people," she carried on.

"My people, you mean French soldiers. Get rid of them! What a stink! They must have gone rotten in transit!"

"No, sir! That smell is normal, they are just ripe, ready to eat, here you try, very good for you," she said as she lifted the lid off one of them.

Minh took a step back and waving his hand turned and left her with a puzzled look on her face. He wondered how someone could even be in the same room as these cheeses. There was no such food in his country!

The morning breeze was sharp and he felt invigorated. Although he missed his friends and family, his heart felt lighter than it had been for a long time. He reached the Town Hall and went straight into the main room where some of the officers were already assembled, sipping their morning coffee—they were talking between themselves about banalities. From time to time laughter would break from the warm murmur that filled the room.

A shy morning sun filtered through the large pains of glass, creating lines of gold which hit the parquet flooring like wide ribbons sent from the heavens. The scent of the coffee and croissant which an elderly woman had brought up on a tray awakened Minh's senses to this new day. He felt sure that things were going to get better. The smell of death which had followed him for so long and had made him retch so many times in the recent past was vanishing in these luxurious surroundings.

He noted the tall ceilings ornate with gold arabesques, the giant paintings of Greek Mythology, the marble mantel piece with its gilded clock.

His eyes met again with a painting of Pandora, whose curiosity got the better of her. He remembered that as she opened the box, out came plagues, misery and mischief, but she managed to shut the lid tight before hope could escape, and that's what Minh lived for now, hope to see the mother land again.

"The sooner the better," he thought to himself.

"Gentlemen," interrupted the colonel, "I have a few things to talk about today. Number one, we've been getting complaints about officers drinking and driving recklessly in town. Number two, officers have been performing unnatural sex acts in local bars and pestering the local girls. VD rate has doubled! This behaviour is immoral and against our code of conduct! So from now on no officer is allowed to go down town without a pass, and keep away from the women. That is it."

As the colonel turned to leave the room, murmur and laughter drifted through the crowd. Minh thought the colonel must be naïve if he thought that abstention in the sex department would be welcomed.

Minh made his way back towards his lodgings.
The farm was a large stone building spread in a U shape. In the yard, ducks and hens roamed freely, pecking at the ground after each wobble. There was a small dip on the side which was always full of water and which gave much pleasure to three geese that competed with the farmer's guard dog.
As he got upstairs to his room, which was small but comfortable, Minh turned the radio on.
"The Allies have regained most of the territories in France, General DeG . . . ."
Minh sat on the bed, which welcomed him with a creak. War was finished. Maybe he could go home now. He wondered if his father was still running the school. He wondered if his mother still made the sesame sweets and the coconut ribbons for his brothers and sisters and if Thao returned home from the forest? Was Tuy still playing with the kite he had left him? What about the horses, the dogs, the corn in the lofts? In his mind a tornado of questions with no answers made him feel dizzy and he lay down for a while.

In the farms around the countryside where they were posted, farmers had to obey new rules. The tables had turned. Minh was happy to close a blind eye from time to time, especially when it was about the killing of stock for food. All farmers had been told that under no circumstances were they to kill their own animals for their supply of meat.
As long as the safety of his battalion was not in jeopardy Minh decided that this was only a small detail. Because of his generosity and fairness, he was respected and treated well by all.

He had noticed that war made people forget their humanity and their sense of decency. On a couple of occasions while walking the streets he had stopped a group of GIs pestering some German girls. He was soon known in the small towns around the Alsace border as "Salomon" because of his assertiveness and his fairness. Although he was not tall, he had an air of assurance, which made him important. His hair and his eyes were jet black. His skin was slightly tanned but not dark. His features were fine and his face smooth and hairless. His knowledge in judo had given him a hidden strength that surprised anyone who tried his luck. His wisdom and his morals came from the Confucius teachings he had received in his father's school.

"The war is finally over!" said one of the soldiers one morning. We've got to report in Grenoble."

As Minh was in his office trying to make sense of what they were supposed to do next, he suddenly realised that he was standing next to a man who had worked for his father. He had not received news from home in such a long time that this warmed his heart.

"News from home is the same as before," the man said to him. "They are still fighting against the Colonialists you know!"

"Have you got fresh news from my father?"

"I'm afraid not. Your brother Thao did not come back after you left. Your father thinks he was probably killed trying to cross the border to the South, away from communist land. That's the last I heard."

"The French have promised us some boats to ship us back. It shouldn't be long now before we see our families again," murmured Minh, remembering his mother in her idyllic garden, the majestic house, his brothers and sisters. How he had missed them!

Months went by and the Vietnamese troops were still waiting. Every time Minh went to inquire about the promised boats, he was told that nothing was in the paper-work about their return home. "Nothing anyone could do about it."

"They have forgotten us!" he declared one evening to his battalion. "They have used us and now we do not exist!"

As the soldiers were beginning to realise that this meant they were stranded, a French officer came in the make-shift room and interrupted their thoughts.

"Get ready, tomorrow is the day!"

"What do you mean? Is it our boat . . . ?" started Minh.

"We are off. Back home!" said one of his comrades.

"You worried for nothing, Minh," said another

"Yes, you have to be patient in situations like this," piped in another, laughing nervously at the thought of the trip home. "They did promise, they couldn't just leave us stranded, could they? We've fought their war, now we've earned some peace," nodded his friend.

The French soldier waved his hands to calm them down.

"Don't get too exited! Your fighting is not over."

"What do you mean?" shouted Minh. "The War is finished!"

"Maybe this war, but back in Vietnam there is another war, in case you had forgotten. The French are having difficulty restraining the Resistance. You are going back to fight the locals."

This was greeted with deafening silence. Their faces showed anger, fear, disbelief, lots of different emotions as they looked at each other for some sort of reassurance.

"I can't believe it!" exclaimed Minh. "How can you ask us to fight our brothers!"

"You belong to the French army now," snapped the officer with a face that disclosed a certain amount of disdain for these "chinks" who were obviously lower grade soldiers. He quickly left the room not interested in what anyone had to say.

In a flash, Minh knew what he had to do.

"Those who do not agree with going back under these conditions come with me."

They all followed him in the office next door where all the files were kept.

"I'm discharging everyone. You are no longer in the army. You are free to go," he said as he was nervously filling out the typed papers and hitting them with a stamp. His anger was reflected in each harsh bang of the stamp on the paper and no-one dared interrupt him.

Once again he would have to be on the run.

The day after, he managed to get a passport as a Member of the International Democratic Youths. It was the 15th of October 1946 and they were on their way to the festival of Prague. As Secretary for the Ho Chi Minh Party, he felt a renewed strength invade his spirit.

"We do not need guns anymore. Every word we print will be like bullets in the head of our enemy!" That was the slogan which was given to him and all his new found friends. The will to go forward all the way to the root of what was costing their country so much young blood was driving them.

Although Minh did not really embrace communism as the ideal supreme power, he decided that these were the only people that could take him closer to his family. He followed them through towns and villages, working on farms, picking the grapes and blowing glass in the factories. He even did some maintenance work on the railway.

"Minh, why are you working so hard?" asked one of his friends one day. "We were looking for you last night. We went to the café, we had a great time. About time we had some relaxation!"

"I need to get home, I told you. I need some money to cross the Russian border."

"You are not still going on about returning to Vietnam, are you?"

"Of course I am, I don't understand why you lot are happy just roaming around these foreign countries."

"We can do more good from here for the mother land, by letting people know the word of Uncle Ho!"

"Well, I need to see my family and I need 18000 francs. Once I am over the Chinese border, it'll be easy."

"You are a dreamer, Minh!" laughed his friend, shaking his head.

"A dream that's coming true! I'm off to Bpect Terespol tomorrow. I'm leaving you the paper-work and the funds I was in charged of."

"Well, good luck, mate!"

His friend was right. Minh realised he needed loads of luck, more than he could imagine.

His long walk to the Russian frontier transformed him into a walking zombie. Time didn't exist anymore. All he did was walk and eat whatever he could steal from the farms he came across. He would spy on the movements within the buildings and when the coast was clear sneak in and grab a loaf or some fruit and eggs that had been left on the kitchen table. He knew he had to keep the money he had saved for the immigration pass. At night, although he had realised that this was the best time to walk away from prying eyes, he would sleep in ditches until dawn or until some passing footsteps woke him.

"I need more money than that!" shouted the guard behind his desk.

Minh felt a weight crushing him. After all that hard work, he still did not have enough to be let through the customs. He suddenly had an idea.

He went to the Russian Communist Party for help.

"Impossible!" exploded the fat man Minh had been sent to. "We need all our funds for the cause. We can't just give to whoever thinks he is in need!"

Discouraged and disappointed by the Party who seemed to preach one thing and do another, he decided he would have no more to do with them.

He left on foot again for Belgium, sleeping in barns and working for his meals.

After several months driven by sheer determination, he managed to locate a friend who had been studying there since before the war and Minh became part of Bui's family.

"My sister wants to marry you!" Bui said to him one day. "I approve."

"Do you, now!" exclaimed Minh laughing, "I'm flattered, but I'm not ready to settle down, you know me! In fact I think I need to go to Paris."

"Paris! Why? Aren't you happy here? I can find you a job and you know you can stay with us as long as you want."

"France's capital will surely offer more opportunities. When I get enough money, I'm going home, I haven't given up yet," he said to Bui just as he was handing him a telegram. "I've managed to get some news for you."

Bui's face was sombre, and Minh read the words that tore at his heart.

"I regret to have to inform you that Nguyen Thi Suu died in 1942 during the Japanese domination of our country. Nguyen Van Hao, her husband died in 1944."

This news had taken five years to reach him! Minh was devastated.

"It is useless trying to understand," murmured his friend, trying to soothe him, "it is war. Mankind is reminded from time to time of his modest origins. Racism and superstitions have contributed to the ravaging of the world and still are."

"You are right. War shows us to what extent the human mind is like lava from a still smouldering volcano that can erupt at any moment," answered Minh trying to fight back the tears that were rushing up to his head. He felt he was going to explode and ran outside.

Digging deep in his pocket for a pencil and a scrap of paper, he sat on the step and started writing. His friend followed him to make sure he was ok. As he looked over his shoulder he could read the scribbles that Minh was putting on paper.

Oh! Why live such a long and laborious life!
Alone and sad, poor and miserable.
The clothes I wear have lost all colour
I am always dreaming unfeasible scenarios
Writing poems, for whom and what purpose?

I think of you my dearest
Not knowing if you think of me
Alone in a painful world
I wait, forever hanging on.

Waiting for whom, waiting for what
Waiting until when, I do not know.
So I write these few words, sending them to the wind
Towards those I love . . .
(The pain of the exiled—Thao)

"Bui, the war has massacred whole families. I've lost my parents, one of my sisters and Thao is still nowhere to be found," murmured Minh. "You know, I feel like a boat without a rudder!"

"Lots of our friends are in the same position. They have left family behind, some had wives and children," answered Bui trying to soothe him by explaining to him that he was not alone in this situation.

"Only Tuy, my younger brother is left to rebuild the family home in the middle of a garden, which is now nothing but rubble."

"At least you still have someone there."

"I feel I will never return now, I have lost everything, even my identity," said Minh as he picked up his pen again.

A slight wind started to shake the leaves above them. They sat down on the stone step that led to the front door. Minh wondered if he was not acting ungrateful towards a friend that had done everything he could to make him welcome in his own home.

"Put it down on paper if it helps you. Your memories, nothing can take them away from you," whispered Bui, as if worried he might disturb.

Minh started to write again.

Yesterday, the flowers were shimmering through the light on the wall.
The leaves and the branches were platted in soft rays of sun.
The gentle breathe would intertwine everything in silent harmony.
Even the moss, brightly coloured, would smile.

But today the sky is sad,
The sky is sad and so am I.
My falling tears will fertilise the earth,
A dried up earth, which endures just like me.

The birds have their nest
And this pains me.

Alone on this strange land,
I dream of the elusive return,
For my body lays here, but my soul is over there.

Boat without a rudder,
When will bitterness fade away?
Around me is but misfortune.
When shall I relive the splendour of my youth?
When will time give me back my soul?

Desperate illusions,
Belated regrets.
My life is gone.
Let's meet the cherished ancestors!

PART THREE

12. East meets West

"I have phoned my uncle at the Vietnamese bank in Paris," said Bui to his pal Minh. "He can help you once you get there. You will need some money and a place to live."

"One day I'll pay you back, you're a friend!"

Minh took Bui's hands in his and they smiled at each other. There was no need for any more words between two who had been so close through hardship.

After packing his few belongings, Minh said his goodbyes. In his bag he still had a gold alarm-clock from his father, a gold pen and some of those precious pictures the family had given him, a little bit yellow and dog-eared from having been looked at so many times.

"I've lost my father's picture!" he whispered to himself, feeling as if another piece of himself had disappeared in the web of time.

As soon as he arrived in Paris he met up with Bui's uncle who gave him some money and an address where he could rent a bed-sit.

It was a small and rather dark room on the top floor of an old stone building. In the summer it was very hot as the ceiling was straight under the rafters. In the winter it seemed colder than outside, but it was home for now.

The person in charge was a round faced young woman with short mousy hair. She was not like any other of the French girls Minh had met before, with their faces covered in make-up, on their high heels, which made them taller in appearance. Marie-Louise was rather masculine in looks.

She was always in trousers and was not afraid of doing all the manual jobs that were needed around the place.

It was that morning as Minh was coming out of the building that he came across her as she was struggling with the large metal bins that had just been emptied.

"Hello, you need some help?"

"I'm ok, thanks. I haven't seen you before," she answered in a firm voice, still dragging the giant container.

"Minh, just moved in. Top floor," he offered.

"I see and what do you do?"

"I found job selling rice, but I wish I could speak better French. Find better job."

"I'm off to the University now, if you want to come. There are lots of your comrades there," she answered invitingly.

Minh decided that he liked her. She was decidedly more interesting that the other females he had met up with.

"Certainly different. Not the norm", he thought.

Her attitude was not flirty but honest. Her stature was strong, rather like her character. Totally different from the girls back home who were very petite and shy.

His limited knowledge of the language would certainly stop him from finding a decent job and he had to do something about this.

"Ok, I follow you. Rice can wait."

As they arrived into the compound of the Sorbonne, he suddenly heard his name.

"Truong! What are you doing here?" he exclaimed as he turned round to meet the familiar face.

"Like you I suppose. Couldn't get back so decided to stay, make the most of it. My family is ok and I will be able to send them some money when I find a job."

"You know my house has been destroyed," said Minh staring at his friend, wondering what his reaction would be.

Truong had been like a brother to him and he knew that he would be saddened by this news.

"God! I'm sorry! Your parents?"

"Gone!" Minh shook his head. He felt choked as the memory returned, like a flood invading a field.

"Come on. Come with us!"

"This is my friend Marie-Louise," suddenly interrupted Minh turning towards the girl who hadn't said a word, listening to the strange singing language she had only heard a few times before.

"Oh, sorry. Hello," said Truong in good French but with a strong Vietnamese accent, turning round to shake the woman's hand.

"She's told me about you lot being here," Minh carried on in Vietnamese.

"I've got to go now, to my lesson," said Marie-Louise smiling. "Might see you tonight?"

"Ok, bye!" waved Minh.

"Oh, I see, you didn't waste time!" teased Truong as their gaze followed the young lady past the different groups of students that dotted the grounds.

"Don't start; I've only just met her! She was dragging the bins from the flat into the yard would you believe."

"Everyone to his own taste. I prefer our dainty feminine girls myself," laughed Truong.

They both went into the building laughing. They were so happy to have found each other again that their worries about home evaporated like the dew in the morning sun.

"Whenever you need money I'm here to help," Truong added just before they entered the class, "You can just owe me a buffalo when we get home, ok?"

Minh laughed, wondering if he would ever get back home, or if he still had some buffalo and horses, or anything to trade with. The last news he had received was grim.

He was glad he had met up with people from his part of the world though and he suddenly felt less lonely. It was as if he had found a part of his family again.

His new friends were in France for all sorts of reasons. Some were there for political reasons; others like him had been stranded in this foreign land. A few had come before the war to study and decided to stay.

The summer soon came with its warm wind and couples started to appear walking along the river Seine. It was on one of these slow walks that Marie-Louise announced to Minh that she had a job in Senegal in a school in Louga.
"School will start in November. I am going back to my parents in Cherbourg, and then I have to prepare for the long journey."
Minh was speechless. This was another blow to him like he had been so used to getting since the war. He was losing somebody close again. They had a good friendship, he thought, but they were just like brother and sister. Of course she had a future and she had to go wherever her career was sending her. He did not know why he felt so lonely.
They parted promising to write from time to time.

The next day Minh got back to his room in the Quartier Latin. As soon as he got onto the landing he realised that the familiar tick-tock of his alarm-clock was not echoing as usual in the grubby stairwell. The door was ajar. He grabbed the broom that was standing in the corner and rushed in brandishing the wooden handle in a defensive position. It was straight away obvious that the thief had long gone. His belongings were all thrown onto the bed in a messy pile, and his alarm-clock was missing.

"I cannot let you the room anymore! You'll have to go, I'll give you your rent back," shouted a woman from the bottom of the stairs.

Minh went onto the landing.

"You talking to me?"

"Of course I am. I don't like your friends, come in here and steal from decent hard-working people. Always get trouble from you immigrants!"

"You wrong! I the one who got robbed!" Minh shouted.

The woman by now had started climbing the wooden steps and was soon in front of Minh, staring him in the face. She had a cigarette stuck in the corner of her mouth and Minh suddenly stepped back wondering if this was a man or a woman. There was no shape to the person who was now confronting him and he could only assume that this was a female because she was dressed in a flowery overall and her hair, which had curlers in, was trying to escape from a chiffon scarf.

Minh left the woman ranting on the landing in search of his friends. They were going to meet at the café later on and he thought he might as well go now rather than have to deal with this demon.

When he came back that evening Minh found his bags on the pavement, and the door was locked.

"One of your friends came to see you the other day," said one of the neighbours being nosy.

"Friend?"

"I don't know, he didn't say his name, one of your race anyway," said the man disdainfully and waving his hand towards Minh. "He robbed the caretaker, you know! Maybe you're in with him. Go on or I'll call the police!"

He understood now why the landlady had been so abrupt with him. She had judged him as "bad" because the robber had been a foreigner.

He went to seek refuge in a church for the night.
Dragging his bag on his shoulder, he climbed the wide steps leading to a tall wooden door. He was yet again "on the street". As he was just about to settle down for the night in one of the confessional boxes, the priest patted him on the back.
"I think you'll be better at my friends in Juvisy. It is called "L'Eau Vive". It is run by Dominicans and they will look after you for free."
"Nothing is free in this world! You even have to pay for your actions . . ."
"You'll just have to work to earn your food."
"What sort of work?"
"Just do some of the cooking or the washing up, nothing too difficult. You understand me?"
Minh nodded. At that moment he decided to burn his papers. He didn't want to bring trouble to his new friends.

The monks were a friendly group but they insisted that he learnt about their religion. Minh who was still writing to Marie-Louise told her about his slow conversion and that he was living in a convent now. Being a strict catholic, she was delighted and offered to be his God-mother.
It was on St John's day in 1948, soon after Christmas that he was baptised and his war name Paul together with the saint's name, gave him his French name, Jean-Paul. A large congregation filled the small church. Minh's closest friends from University were there and Dominican fathers arrived from Saulchoir. Even the Ambassador of Canada, who had heard about the conversion, had sent some sugared almonds,

as it is customary for a christening. Minh hadn't felt so much at peace for a long time. Marie-Louise had asked one of her friends to stand in for her. She had asked her parents, who were in Paris at the time, to make themselves known to the monks and to meet her dear friend Jean-Paul. She had told them how they had met and how he was so different from other boys she had met before and more importantly how he had converted to Catholicism and this had really impressed them.

One lunch time as Minh was peeling the potatoes, he heard some commotion in the corridor. Soon a uniformed man barged into the kitchen.

"We are looking for a deserter!" he exclaimed, pushing past the robed man who was trying to stop him in his tracks.

"We have no deserters here, officer. Whatever gave you that idea!" exclaimed the Dominican.

"We have been informed that a stranger is working for you, a foreigner," said the man as he came in front of the cook and added, "What are you doing with that knife?"

"Can't you see!" Minh answered with moderation as the officer was starting a meticulous inspection of the bins.

"I want to see all your correspondence and papers."

"I am really sorry, but any papers I had, I had to use in the WC."

"Don't be cocky with me chinky! What's your name? Not Paul by any chance!"

"Paul? How can I be Paul, I am Vietnamese, just a cook. This name does not exist in my country."

"Were you ever in the French army?"

"What did this Paul do?" interrupted the man of the cloth with a worried look on his face. "The war ended four years ago."

"He signed the demobilisation papers for a whole battalion. Their commandant was apparently somewhat embarrassed when he realised he had no-one to carry out his orders," smirked the police man as he left the premises, obviously not really bothered. He was only doing a job.

When the officer had gone Minh explained what had happened and why he had freed his friends from their military duties and although he had the support of his new friends, he did not feel safe anymore. He had to go on the run again.

"Why do people always think that because you are a foreigner you automatically are the one at fault?"

"Men only see in others what they are themselves, my friend," murmured the monk.

13. Looking for love

He still had the photographs in his pocket, a minute taste from his past.

He studied the dog-eared picture of his mother in her straw hat, his aunt Hue, his younger sister Thi and his brother Tuy. He could not read the faded words without crying at the memories they brought back. He felt that when someone died it was a little bit of that memory that left too.

Some of the souvenirs started to merge into one and the edges were less defined.

Blurry eyed Minh read,

"Three years, you are only fifteen. It seems an eternity, but time will go quickly, and when you come back everything will have changed," his mother had written.

"Terrible separation of the blood! Maybe as you gaze at this picture you will think of returning to us, and make everything as it was before, Thi Duc."

"Keep these pictures near you, and when you look at them think of your country and come straight back to your family in Asia. Although it causes heart ache now, all is well as long as the hope of seeing each other again one day is present, Thi"

"Today I say goodbye, but soon I will say hello, Tuy."

On the back of the last picture he had received more recently through a friend, he scanned the words that he knew by heart,

"Meeting: we were there, we came on several occasion, but the peach blossoms have fallen many times, and you still have not returned, Aunt Hue"

Minh thought of Thao, whose disappearance was the reason for him to be here in this foreign country. He didn't blame him at all. He just wondered where he was, maybe in the Huon forest, where the birds were flying free. His brother's ghost was present in his dreams and always whispered to him in the stillness of the nights.

"Where the faithful river murmurs at the same place as before, it is there whatever happens, that you will find me"

"I have no tolerance for those who, to survive, have chosen to merge into this society where I find myself like a prisoner. Lots of our old friends have buried their past and their culture, like old tools in the shed at the bottom of the garden!" Minh exclaimed to Vinh, a new acquaintance.

"You won't let go of the past, that's why you cannot carry on living. You feel bitter, neither this nor anything else will get your parents back!"

"I haven't received any news from home for a long time. Until now I had some money, enough to survive in Paris. This town feels to me like an immense island surrounded by the fury of a gale."

"And I tell you again that this is because you will not let things rest. Why can't you make the most of what you have now? You have friends, they will help you, and you know that. Getting on with things does not mean that you forget the past."

"I met someone, but she left to work abroad. I've lost contact."

"Hold on! Someone was asking this morning for a Jean-Paul. Isn't that your French name? A letter from Senegal he said."

"It's for me! Who brought the letter?" Minh exclaimed, finding it difficult to control himself and jumping to his feet.

"Some monk I think, from the looks of his cloak. I think he left it with Lao."

Minh ran all the way to Lao's rooms.

They were living at a Youth Club, a run-down building with small dingy rooms each side of a narrow and dark corridor. They were given three meals a day, if you could call them meals, but at least they did not starve. It was charity run and the lodgers were of all nationalities, most of them jobless or on meagre wages.

Minh reached room number 15 and burst in.

"Lao!"

"Yes, I know, here it is!" sung Lao handing him the letter edged with the tricolour lines.

Minh ran back to the privacy of his room and tore open the letter.

"My dear Jean-Paul,

I haven't received any news from you for a long time now and I wonder if you are all right. I heard that you have left the convent and I am really worried about you.

There is not one day that I do not think of you. I am very proud of you entering into our Christian family. I am only sad that I was unable to be there with you on your big day, although Jeanette, our mutual friend, agreed to represent me. I would love for you to come over to Senegal. I have told my parents about you, and how you have lost your parents.

As you know I still work in St Louis at the convent. I am hoping to get my own lodgings soon. Sharing a room with someone else is not ideal.

The weather is always hot, thirty three degrees during the day and twenty five at night. Although it gives me palpitations, I think you might like it as it might be close to what you were used to in your country.

I am the only one here to be Bachelor in Philosophy and so as well as being in charge of the top classes, they have asked me to be on the board of Governors and on the examination jury.

If you came, we could find you a job in the neighbouring town. I have a friend who can put you up in St Louis. My contract is for three years, and already one year has gone by. You are my god-son and I will help you as much as I can, but it is up to you.

Please God this letter will find you well.

Marie-Louise."

Minh took his pen and wrote what he felt in his heart.

"My dearest Marie Louise,

I am now at 24 rue Mouffetard, since April 49. It is not very nice, but it is a roof over my head. I am looking for a job and when I do find one, I will be able to afford better.

Thank you for thinking of me, your god-son. I was baptised Jean-Paul, Antoine, Louis in December 48 at L'Eau Vive, Soisy sur Seine, on the Sunday after Christmas.

I feel nearer to you and stronger, but I still carry, deep within me, a profound sense of solitude. As soon as I do not think of God, I feel abandoned in the midst of men. I realise how unstable my life is, and always aspire towards inner peace.

You are so far away!

I saw you and I loved you.

When you left my heart broke and I feel my life is finished!

Jean Paul"

A month later he received an answer from "his girl", who advised him to leave Rue Mouffetard, as it was well known for its bad reputation.

With the help of his Dominican friends he found new lodgings at rue de la Montagne.

"I want to open a home for Vietnamese orphans in Juvisy. Minh, do you think you could run it for me," asked Father Gagneux one June morning.

"Of course, I think it is an excellent idea," nodded Minh to the elderly man in front of him.

Life was like that. There were moments when several routes opened to you and you had to choose between them. They did not lead to the same place and did not offer the same trip. Only the future, which in no way could be seen at the time, would reveal if you had made the right choice.

He felt he had not had many joyful moments since the war. He had been unhappy like those who had nothing left except their memories. He often had the uneasy feeling that he already was a ghost, one of those lost souls who are looking for some ephemeral happiness.

The sun was playing in the leaves above the group of small tables where they had decided to sit for a chat, making a lacy pattern on the white cloths. Minh fell deeper into his daydream as if hypnotised by the patches of brightness.

Maybe life was not all bad. Maybe he was on this Earth to help others, stranded like him far away from home. Like everybody he yearned for love because life was impossible without love.

Father Gagneux had been to Vietnam. He knew his people and understood their customs. These were not savages as most in the West imagined, but educated people, governed by very high morals. He understood why they did not agree with the French.

"The only people who want help from the West in your country, are the politicians in Saigon," said his friend.

"That's right, because they are getting rich with the help of their new friends!" Minh's voice showed a certain amount of anger.

"You know the anti-colonialist revolution is still at its strongest."

"I know. They said they'd ship us back if we agreed to fight against our own!"

"No way!" exclaimed Father Gagneux.

"They can't deal with it themselves because the North is using mercenaries. It is "the enemy without a face", so they thought they'd use us. The country is divided into two."

"Apparently, Mendes France will sell the South to the Americans! Here, look, that's what the papers say."

"You know that the Franco-Vietnamese problem only stemmed from the fact that we wanted our independence, not because we didn't want the French influence anymore," said Minh, putting the paper aside.

"Didn't the Vietnamese ever want the French out?"

"Of course some did, but on the whole they appreciated having a teacher. Lots of French customs have been adopted."

"The Roman alphabet for one . . ." nodded the father.

"That's right; all the Vietnamese want is a place in the government of their country. It's only fair, don't you think!"

"Totally agree! They should at least have an equal partnership. Stuart Mills said that "what makes a civilised society is when the members accept their limitations within their respective activities". The French have not been fair at all in their running of their colonies, but then what country has!" He started fiddling with the handle of his cup where a tea as yellow as honey was still waiting to be drunk.

"What went wrong is that they wanted to change things too quickly. The morale of Confucius and the cult of the ancestors have guided Vietnam for millions of years, what did they expect? You cannot change overnight how someone thinks and breathes!" exclaimed Minh, forgetting that the person facing him was totally in agreement.

"I know a Confucian is master of his passions, whereas the French have no reserve. It must have been a shock for your people."

"There could not have been anything more brutal! The East loses itself in contemplative meditation whereas the West follows Science and Technology. Totally different way of seeing things."

"What I think sums it all is that respect for others is being replaced by the individual right," observed the priest.

"Well, not all change is bad, I must admit. I was attracted by the new like most of my friends. My father was totally against it though," agreed Minh.

Minh thought of Marie-Louise, the French girl who had turned his head. What would his father have said? Deep down he felt something calling him, far away from here, on another continent.

14. Rebirth in Africa

In Oct 49 Paul arrived on Marie-Louise's doorstep.

He had decided that he would take a plane towards his destiny.

Just like parallel streams would suddenly join a great river, they were meeting again amidst the river of humanity.

"Promise me that we will not be parted again," pleaded Minh as they embraced in the small yard surrounding her lodgings that she was sharing with the other teachers.

"No, we won't. I will help you all I can to repair the hurt that you have suffered. I have lots of nice friends and they will be your friends too. You will not be lonely anymore. You'll see, St Louis is a nice place."

Marie-Louise mentioned the daughters of her dear friend the Administrator of Louga, saying that one of them would make a good wife for "my Paul", as she called him, for this was his war name. To his disappointment he realised that she had not noticed that it was her he wanted to marry.

"You can't live here. The nuns are already gossiping about the fact that I go out more than I used to and they even wrote to my parents about it," she said, interrupting his thoughts.

"What do you mean? Aren't you allowed to go out?"

"Yes, of course I am. It's just that the first year, I didn't know many people and so I stayed in, reading or writing rather than go down town like the others. They automatically assumed I was perfect material to become a nun!"

"Did they ask your parents to decide for you to become a nun?" Minh enquired.

"No, my parents could not decide for me! I am religious but I could not become like those nuns. They have vicious tongues when they want to. They told my parents that because I was going out quite often to see my friends in the evening, I should be careful about getting a bad reputation."

"Oh, and they think they will get close to their God by spreading rumours!" Minh exclaimed.

"Don't worry, I am due to get some lodgings from the government and when I get my own place you can move in with me. We will have more privacy."

"That's good from this government to help people like that!"

"All teachers coming from France to the colonies are entitled to a place to live. I'll be glad to be out of here . . . anyway for now you will stay at my friend Mr Besnard. He has three daughters. They are really nice people and I am sure you will be well looked after."

Minh let himself be shown his new surroundings, another continent and another way of life.

He had noticed his photo on her desk, and he understood straight away that she had been longing to see him again, but he felt that he was to her like a brother in distress who needed help. And she had just decided that her goal in life was to remedy this.

"I have written to my parents about you. Did they come to see you in Paris?" asked Marie Louise, while sorting out some paperwork that lay in a pile on the desk.

"Yes, thank you so much for the silver cross too."

"I wanted to show that your god-mother was thinking about you. I had the date of your baptism inscribed on it, did you notice?" Her eyes met his over the books.

"It was very nice of you to think of me. I did feel less lonely when I realised that you had not forgotten me."

"I know you miss your parents and although no-one will ever replace them I will help fill that void."

Again Minh felt his heart sink. How could he make her understand how he felt without frightening her away? She only thought that he was missing his parents, his family and his country. She saw him as a challenge to her generous nature, but not as part of her life. He did not dare open his heart to her yet and it pained him to see that she did not feel the same intense feeling he had experienced from the day he had seen her outside their flat in Paris.

He tried to suppress that feeling from then on. He had taken on board her God, in an attempt to get closer to her. Now he was sharing with her everyday problems and also successes. It was a painful process, trying to gain her love in slow steps as he was yearning for the moment when she would reach towards the light of sudden realisation. What if she did love him after all, not with the love of a companion but the love of a lover?

Minh knew in the depth of his soul that he wanted to be one with this woman who had awakened within him a sensation he had not felt before. From now on he would be guided by his heart. This new feeling was giving him a new strength. It was giving him wings. He felt he could accomplish anything, here next to her, he would start living again.

She was the only one who had not noticed the closeness they displayed in front of company and everyone around started talking about the white woman who had a Chinese lover.

"My parents are worried," she said one day to Paul as she was handing him the vegetables for the dish he was preparing for their supper. "I must tell them that you are in fact living at my friend's the Administrator and that he has three daughters living there too. You know, they would all make very good wives . . . isn't there one you like?"

"I know that there is no way I can marry you," Paul interrupted her, putting the knife down and wiping his hands on a towel. "I am poor and I must marry a woman who is poor just like me."

"Oh, no, Paul, this has nothing to do with material things. I am your God-mother and because of this I don't think I would be allowed to marry you," she explained, moving closer to him.

"But why not if you love me. I think you do, otherwise why have you helped me so much?" he murmured gingerly.

"I know you are a catholic now, my parents would not be able to say anything about you being a different religion . . ." she said staring at him.

"As you know my father was a Confucian, but did you know that my mother was a Christian? We have always been taught to respect other religions."

"Well, I . . . I like you very much. In fact there is no one else like you in my life. I just don't think I am the marrying kind," she carried on, as if talking to herself, in a world of her own, searching her soul for her true feelings.

"Do you know our children would be very good looking? That's how it is with mixed bloods. But I don't want to upset your parents; they were so kind to me in Paris. Ultimately, you must do what they want, that is the Confucian way of my father."

Marie-Louise looked up and was speechless for a while, staring at his young face.

"Your hair is so dark that it reminds me of ebony. Your eyes, the shape of almonds, are bright and true. Your skin is smooth, without a blemish," he heard her murmur.

The realisation suddenly widened her eyes. He knew she wanted to embrace him, but he understood that governed by the reserve she had been accustomed to, she did not put her mouth on his as she wanted to, she just grabbed his hand and squeezed it tight. Her eyes were misting over as she was overcome by this new sensation of a love, which took them suddenly away from their surroundings and placed them on their own in the world. They felt free. They were one.

"You know, a meeting is always the fruit of a celestial choice," he whispered.

The intense emotion on her face showed the turmoil that her new state of mind provoked within her.

"I did not look for that. I did not think this would ever happen to me," she exclaimed unsettled.

"It was sudden for me too. It was love at first sight. When fortune decides on blind love, water and mountain meet. Love transforms people. Before and after you are not the same. The love I feel surpasses my beliefs. I was Confucian and you are Christian like my mother. I respected your beliefs and your opinions, I waited for you. This respect for others is part of the compassion of the Buddha."

He then wrapped her up into their first embrace.

For Christmas, two months after his arrival, Marie-Louise was granted an apartment in Louga.

The two rooms were wide and bright, which contrasted with where she had been before. She invited Jean-Paul to share her lodgings on a platonic basis. It was like a breath of fresh air to be free from prying eyes and the gossipy nuns. They celebrated with a bottle of wine which they drank standing on the small balcony. From there they overlooked the town. They felt part of it but at the same time away from its hustle and bustle. On the horizon the sun was playing tricks with the roofs, colouring the sky with carmine and gold.

Now they had to think of a way for Minh to get a regular income. The small jobs he did in restaurants were not very lucrative. Marie-Louise who had been sending money over to France to help her brother and older sister didn't want to stop doing this straight away, but her salary would not stretch anymore.

One day she arrived home full of excitement.
"I have been offered several hectares of land for a reasonable price. We could keep goats and grow bananas. You could look after them."
"I don't think we should stay in this country," he announced, morose.
"Have you had trouble at the restaurant again?" she asked as her face dropped.
"That stupid woman, she thinks I am a spy!"
"A spy! What ever gave her that idea?"
"You know I had trouble with the police in France over the papers I signed to release my battalion; I am worried she might cause more trouble."
"How would she know about that?"
"I don't think she knows, she thinks I am here to spy on her exorbitant prices, but this could attract trouble for me and you."
"If we get married one day, we will go back to France," she suddenly declared.
He stared into her eyes. He had not mentioned marriage for a long time. His heart suddenly filled with emotion. He grabbed her.
"The mix of race makes new cultures, more refined and more complex than those they come from you know. We will have beautiful children!" he whispered in her hair.

He realised that it was the small idiosyncrasies that made her precious to him. It was the little things that only the two of them knew about each other, that made them soul mates.

"Paul, you keep saying about children . . ." she ventured. "I am not dainty like the women in your country, I am even wondering if I can have children!" Then she added: "my character is very masculine and forceful, I know that, I've been told often enough and I don't mind it, but how can you love me? My past is far from perfect."

"You don't love someone because they are perfect, you love them in spite of the fact that they are not. I have a very tumultuous past as well, which could catch up on me and attract trouble for you too. That is why so often I have thought that I was not worthy of your love and that your parents were right to warn you against a mixed marriage," he stated, studying her face and waiting for her reaction.

"I think we have to avoid weighing the pro and con of our acts. Regrets are what is the most destructive in human nature," she declared.

"If I had known the consequences of my actions I would have chosen a different path," Minh nodded.

"Well, to imagine what ones life could have been is a futile exercise. It's better to look at the future and not look at yesterday with regrets. If you had not decided to come instead of your brother, we would have never met . . ." she smiled.

Minh gave her smile back. He was sure he had found his soul mate. Someone he could trust and understood how he felt and someone he understood too.

Sometimes he felt a yearning to tell her about his family, about a life that seemed so far away now. He had found her, but some days she was not enough to fill the enormous void in his life. He had tried to get in touch with his younger brother Tuy on several occasions, but the letters kept coming back unopened.

At times everything seemed to be fading away. The ancestors' tombs were disappearing into the earth and there was nobody left to tell and nothing left to tell about.

His days were not too bad, but the nights were hell. The dreams of death still oppressed him, and the unseen fear kept him bouncing out of bed. On these nights he had to have a drink to help him drown the ghosts of the past. The alcoholic drink helped him sleep. Night after night he tried the same trick and it seemed to work although he had to drink a little bit more each time to do the job. On occasions he would anesthetize himself in bars. He knew Marie-Louise was being patient with him. She had told him that the way he felt would change once they had their own family.

His world often seemed like a featureless world and he was evading it by writing endless poems.

"Maybe I have no right to ask you to marry me. I still want to go back home one day. I feel I will not rest until then," he would say to her.

"When we have children, you might feel different," she repeated. "Anyway, how can you go back when your country is still at war? It is too dangerous."

"It is America's and China's war not ours. If we had been left alone it wouldn't have gone on for so long. If it goes on much longer, it will be impossible for anyone to recover!" Marie-Louise cradled him and he felt himself relax.

"I am keeping the tears for the day, when once again, my feet will feel the native soil, and they will be tears of joy," he murmured.

15. Tuy's War

"Do you know that the Emperor Bao Dai is my cousin?"

"What do you mean?" exclaimed Marie-Louise.

"My ancestors were the Emperors of Annam."

"Do you mean you are a prince and your family lost everything because of the French!"

"No, not quite. The throne went to our cousins because a son died before his father. So the emperor's line got sort of shifted."

"But then, can't you use your connections to get a good job, a good position in life?"

"I could enter the world of politics, but Father Gagneux told me that politic is not something for a Christian person. On top of that Bao Dai is working for the Americans and I do not agree with the way the US wants to deal with the conflict in Vietnam," explained Minh.

"I see what you mean, but sometimes you have to swallow your pride. I was involved in politics when I was at University in 45 you know. Mind you, I think that has proved bad for me too. I had difficulties getting accepted here. People do not trust you. They think you will attract trouble."

"People judge on appearances!"

"That is what I told my parents, not to judge on appearances. I have decided to go back to France after taking my Teaching Certificate and we can get married then," she stated proud of herself.

"I really don't want to cause trouble in your family. I have nothing to give you. The little I had I gave away. I think I should go back to Paris to find a job. Then if we still feel the same we can get married," he insisted.

She nodded, then looking at the floor she started . . .

"I should be finished here next May, if I can get a boat back, then we can have a treble marriage ceremony!" She looked at him for acknowledgement. "My younger sister and my brother are getting hitched too! I will tell my parents that I am not marrying just anybody . . ."

"What good is it to say that I am a prince," he said shrugging his shoulders, "all I had I have lost, even my name. What good is it to recount such things, who would believe them anyway?"

"I believe you. I knew you were not just anybody, that you had education, by the way you acted and the way you were thinking. I have told my parents that they should not be prejudiced."

"As I said, I think I will be better off in Paris. The weather here does not agree with me, it is too dry, not like the heat in Hue, which is damp."

"Unfortunately, I am not allowed to leave here without the authorisation of the governor," she said wide eyed.

"I know. I don't want you to stop what you have started here anyway. You must finish, and then come to me in Paris when the time is right. We can then prove to your parents that this was not just a fling."

It was not until June 51 that Marie-Louise got back to France. She met up with her Jean-Paul, as he was known by her family, for it was his Christian name, and they got married in September with the blessing of her parents. Minh was happy to have been accepted into this caring family. The reception was at his friend's Ngo Quang, in Ablon, where he had worked in his Nuoc Mam factory, making the typical Vietnamese fish sauce. Though only a few chosen guests had been invited it was a grand affair where European and Eastern Asian ways mixed beautifully in a whirl of colours and fragrances.

Minh had finally received news from Tuy through the Red Cross. The main house had been destroyed several times, but each time Tuy had managed to rebuild it as best he could. He and his wife were still living in it with their son. To think that his parents' home was still there warmed his heart. He could imagine them more easily, in surroundings he knew well. At the same time deep down, he understood that the countryside must be quite different now from the idyllic setting of his youth. He knew it would be scarred by the bombings, which had been the worst in the region around Hue where they lived. Tuy could not say much in his letters as these were censored, and Minh didn't ask because he did not want to cause trouble.

In 1952 Minh got a job as Secretary for the Diplomatic Corps for his Majesty Bao Dai at the Vietnamese Embassy in Paris. That same year he was officially relieved of his duties to the French Government.

On his papers was written: "Did not ask to be repatriated within the right time limit."

"Typical! It is never their fault is it?" exclaimed Minh as he waved the paper at Marie-Louise.

"I know, calm down. At least you have a good life here now. You've met up with some good people who want the best for you."

"It's only taken them seven years to acknowledge us. All those, who did their dirty work and didn't want to fight their brothers," he carried on, not paying attention to her.

Minh went into the bedroom, lay on the double bed and stared at the ceiling.

They had managed with the help of her parents to buy a nice two bedroom flat with balcony on the outskirts of Paris. It was modern and bright and a far cry from the two rooms they had had at the beginning rue Lantiers in the 17th Arondissement.

Minh felt he should be more grateful, for destiny had plucked him from nothing and given him back a chance. He had a good job and a second child on the way. What else could a man ask for?

Marie-Louise had started teaching again as her parents had offered to look after their baby daughter.

"Happiness can only exist in parallel to unhappiness," he thought.

One day Minh came into their apartment very agitated.

"You know my position at the Embassy is very precarious. The situation in Vietnam is very unsettled. Ngo Dinh Diem is a very energetic man. He is against any foreign interference and after 80 years of French colonisation he is about to proclaim a Republic,"

"What's going to happen to Bao Dai! He is still the Emperor?"

"He's gone to Cannes," replied Minh shaking his head. "Diem has sent him an ultimatum; he's given him forty eight hours to go back or he loses the throne."

"He won't be able to go back in such a short time!"

"That's right. Diem will be Prime Minister. He'll be in charge of the South, but the Republic will be far from stable."

"How do you mean?"

"Do you think that those who have tasted the riches of the West will want to go back to fight at his side? Then there is America lurking in the background, and they don't realise that it is a psychological error to ask the Vietnamese to fight against communism before they have their independence. The Vietnamese will take any offer available to achieve their goal, which is freedom. People die for their dreams you know."

"Do you think your brother and his family will be OK?

"They'll survive. The Vietnamese are hard-working opinionated people. They seem passive but they are full of vitality. They have a sort of energy that nothing can weaken. Through all the set-backs and defeats they have never tired of pursuing their goal."

"Some people say that they are too passive. They have never known independence and yet they carried on through the ages being subdued," Marie-Louise ventured.

"They might seem passive to you, but they have a lot of tenacity and a very strong national spirit. Their energy is strong but supple, patient and insinuating. The road they will take in order to obtain their goal may not be the most direct, but they will not stop until they get there, you'll see. Their energy is like a bamboo in a storm; it looks fragile but is extremely robust."

Minh thought of his brother's letters and the news of glad and sad tidings. He could read between the lines. Tuy had rebuilt the house so many times, he had forgotten how many. He had placed the tablets of the ancestors up to be worshipped at feast days on the only piece of furniture they had left, a large dark oak chest, which stood proud in the middle of the room. To the side was a double bed and above it were the coffins for him and his wife. He had spoken to his son, for he had chosen where his place in the earth should be when the time came. It was to be next to his parents, who he had put next to his grandparents. He had gathered many of the ancestors' bones, which had been scattered by the war. They were now all in the field above the main house and were waiting for the wall to be built around them, so the evil spirits would pass them by and not disturb their rest. Only little mounds of earth lay there at the moment and a handful of spent incense sticks marked the spots.

Minh pondered for a while and then murmured pensively: "Only my brother is left now. I will be next to join the ancestors."

"Don't be silly," observed Marie-Louise, "you are still young, many others will go before you!"

"I tell you, I will soon die without having seen the mother land again. What good is it to say that you are a prince—we all end up the same way."

"Don't feel blue! What can I do to make you feel better? I have tried everything in my power not to make you forget, but to help you accept your new life," she explained patiently.

"I know I'm not being fair to you. It's just that sometimes I think that even God has something against the Asiatic!"

"Don't be paranoid. I know you had a sad life but there are always those worse off than you—remember that." She rubbed his shoulders to wipe away his sorrow.

Epilogue

Minh worked for the Vietnamese Embassy until 1965, when the Old Regime was overthrown. His redundancy was a terrible blow to him and his depression grew worse. He was not a person who could stay idle for long, but his lack of fluency in the French language, even after all those years in the country, stopped him from finding a job other than in restaurants after that. Although a great cook, he missed the world of Politics and used to spend his spare time writing endless essays and poems in Vietnamese. Unfortunately these were lost before they could be translated.

The story of Nguyen Van Minh might seem difficult to accept in some of its details, as a lot of facts have been clouded over by the complexities of historical events, which entwine them. It takes place in Vietnam the "land of the lake", in the area around Hue, which was known as Annam.

Vietnam is a band of earth restricted to the North by China, to the South and the East by the sea and to the West by the Annamic Range. It was coveted by many for its ideal geographical position.

During the Prehistoric Era, the Viet, who were a Chinese ethnic group, were pushed back towards the South and had to take shelter in the territory of Siam. Later on with the alliance of a Vietnamese princess to a Siamese prince, Vietnam gained Cochin—China, which was to the South of the peninsula.

The Chinese had made a protectorate of Annam, which was the land around Hue and although they only owned it in a symbolic way, they then sold it to the French. The name Annam was given by the Chinese who had reorganised the general government. The French used that same name to describe the region bound to the North by Tonkin and to the South by Cochinchina.

The Vietnamese preferred the ancient name of Viet, meaning "far away", indicating a state far away in relation to the capital of the Empire of China. The word Nam meaning "South of the Middle Empire", the name Viet-Nam symbolised the national unity Emperor Gia Long had achieved throughout the whole of his kingdom at the beginning of the last century. The social organisation was founded on the feudal aristocracy.

Vietnam was divided into three provinces called the Ky, or domains, which were each governed by a Viceroy. The Viceroy had above him the King of Annam who had the title of Emperor. The Vice-Roy called upon Mandarins to govern several districts.

The Nguyen Dynasty started with the Acquisition of Cambodia. It is under that dynasty that Hue became the capital of Vietnam in 1658.

The Vietnamese name consists of three words, the family name, the middle tag, which denotes whether it is male of female, the age and the social status, and the first name.

"Văn" means "scholar and denotes that it is a male. "Thị" denotes a female. The first name is in fact the title and differentiates one person from another.

On top of their birth names the Emperors had a ruler's name which often makes it a nightmare for the genealogists to make sense of their findings.

Amongst the lower classes the child might receive the name of the year, or the name of the village where he was born. The more cultured classes may choose a more poetic name. At home these names might be replaced by nick-names chosen on account of the talents or habits of each child. A girl might for example be called sister and her number within the family. This custom extends to the servants too and a maid becomes the sister of her master's servants.

There were four social classes, the Mandarins who were scholars and "gave the world thought and order", the craftsmen, which "created tools for their livelihood", the farmers who "gave the world food" and the shopkeepers who "produced nothing but money for themselves". The Mandarins were hereditary Mandarins and were landowners.

The property where a Mandarin lived accounted for several houses on the same plot of land, which was occupied by members of the family. These detached houses were on one level and had several rooms. Sometimes a water-clock called a "clepsydra" could be found in the main room.

The workers lived in a hut built with daub and covered with rice straw. Those living in the mountains had bamboo houses built on stilts to prevent animals from walking in.

In high society a man was allowed to have a second wife but only if his wife had not given him any children, and she would be asked for her approval. The second wife would have a lower status. The Emperor Thanh Thai, Emperor

Tu-Duc's nephew, abolished the royal harem between 1889 and 1907.

Under the Nguyen dynasty, the state religion was Confucianism, now the religious question is a very complicated one. After the invasions and where so many people have converged, Vietnam is a country of mixed religions. In one pagoda you may see some inscriptions leading you to believe that you are in a temple dedicated to Sky and Earth, an essential agricultural cult, which was imported from China by the Emperors, but at the same time you may notice a statue of Buddha on the main altar. Religions whether they are used pure or mixed by each individual are not enough to satisfy the Vietnamese need for supernatural comfort. In this country where the customs are harsh as Nature itself, many feel an intense need for support and consolation. The Vietnamese, although on the surface an optimist, believes he is constantly pursued by bad luck. He feels menaced by tigers, fevers, debtors and even his neighbours. Life appears unstable, and man is in constant fear of a future that seems to him ever so dark. He will turn and find comfort in front of fortune tellers. Deep down the true religion of the Vietnamese is the devotion to the soul of the ancestors. He uses sticks of incense and offers them in prostration on the altar of the ancestors in the same way as on the altar of Buddha. Every dwelling, no matter how poor, has a shrine devoted to the ancestors.

Confucius' moral was the intellectual's religion. It started in 11 BC and was the teaching of restraint and the three bonds of subordination that form the basis of society: man to ruler, woman to man and son to father.

Its principals are based on charity and respect for the ancestors. That is why in every house the ancestors are honoured with the burning of incense.

High society funerals lasted three months, for the poor, fifteen days to one month. The bearers would put a glass full of water on top of the coffin as they carried it to its last resting place. Contrary to common belief this was no superstition. They were paid depending on the amount of water they had spilled. The wooden box had to be carried with great care and respect for the deceased.

Ancestor worship was essentially a very important family affair. The funeral procession passed in front of the person's house, which was decorated with multicoloured paper lanterns. More lanterns, on which the name of the deceased was written, preceded the coffin and were decorated with ribbons on which Chinese characters described his origins and his virtues. The close family dressed with un-hemmed clothes to show denial for the material world.

The size of the tomb depended on the person's fortune and the burial site was chosen before his death. The poor only had a mound of dirt to show where they lay, while the rich would have a monument surrounded by a wall with columns brightly decorated with dragons and inscriptions. A stone called the bing-phong protected the entrance from the bad spirits.

The French invaded Vietnam in 1859 but their governors had difficulty finding princes to accept to act as their "puppet". Lots of emperors were assassinated in palace intrigues or were exiled in France and North Africa where they lived under surveillance.

In 1885, Ham Nghi, Emperor Bao Dai's great uncle, was the last legitimate Emperor of the Nguyen dynasty. The "wandering king" still governed for five years from his hidden retreat until he was exiled to Algers by the French.

At the beginning of the Second World War, France enrolled the young Indochinese to boost their army numbers. Nguyễn Văn Minh, my father, was one of those young men enlisted to fight in the French army in 1939. He was the second son of Nguyễn Văn Hao and Nguyễn Thị Sưu, who lived with their five children just North of Hue in the province of Quang Binh. Today the youngest of the five, Tuy, is the only one still burning the incense on the ancestor's shrine.

All his life Minh (enlisted as Thao, his elder brother) or known in France as Jean Paul, my father, dreamed of returning home. He was a very modest and lonely man,
In 1949, the French Government was still looking for Paul. He escaped the prying eyes of the military police by going to Senegal where our mother was teaching. Back in Paris they married in 1951 and had four children.

After years of waiting for the new Vietnamese government to give him permission to go back to the land of the ancestors, Minh received his visa six month after his death in 1976. The war broke his spirit.
I wish I had known him better.